GOD'S
FORGIVENESS

Also available from Bruce M. Bumgardner

Bruce has hundreds of hours of Bible teaching available online.

These audio tools are indepth, line-by-line Bible studies.

For a complete list of Bible studies available simply go to our website.

There is no charge for any of these lessons.

www.ourpvbc.org

GOD'S
FORGIVENESS

Sharing God's Perfect Peace

Bruce M. Bumgardner

Published By

Jericho PRESS

Leading the Way Back to the Bible

God's Forgiveness
by Bruce M. Bumgardner

ISBN: 978-1-935222-25-5

Published by Jericho Press
Nashville, TN

Additional copies may be obtained through
Grace Evangelistic Ministries
GEMworldwide.org

Printed in the United States of America

Dedication

This book is dedicated to my family, and to the people of Pine Valley Bible Church, past and present, who have been such a source of encouragement, blessing and love to me over the years.

Soli Deo Gloria

Acknowledgments

My profound thanks go to Debby Hagar and Richard Hays for their tireless help with the manuscript and encouragement to complete the project. Without that encouragement I doubt this book would have ever been written.

I would also like to express my sincere gratitude to Robb Beyer for sharing his considerable expertise in putting the final product together and getting it ready to publish. Robb's skill in this area is unmatched and I feel privileged that he took an intense interest in making this work the best it could be.

I am also most appreciative of the efforts of Linda and Ken Monroe, Greg Ford, Cyndy Bumgardner, Marcia Bumgardner, Robert Hernandez, Richard Simon and Geri Beyer in editing the manuscript and suggesting helpful changes. This is time consuming work and I give you my sincere thanks.

While there have been many men who have influenced me greatly in my theological education and time in ministry, two are deserving special mention here: Robert Lightner and Elliot Johnson, both professors at Dallas Theological Seminary. Dr. Lightner taught me how to hold to strong theological views with kindness and grace. Dr. Johnson taught me how to properly interpret the Scriptures and to lead with humility and gentleness. Thank you both. I admit I am still a work in progress.

I am overwhelmingly grateful to God for His providence in partnering me in ministry with Moses Onwubiko. We have been blessed to minister together on every continent (except Antarctica) in dozens of countries. It is an honor to be associated in ministry with you and Grace Evangelistic Ministries. Thank you, Moses.

And finally, I am eternally grateful to my Lord Jesus Christ, who gave His life for me, providing for my forgiveness, so that I could live with Him forever. You are my Creator, Savior and Sustainer. Thank you for calling me Your own.

Table of Contents

A Sunday Morning in Africa

I had just finished preaching on a warm and rainy morning in Port Harcourt, Nigeria. As I was making my way though a group of people who were encouraging me and wishing me a safe journey back to the U.S. later that afternoon, I was introduced to a man who asked if he could have a moment in private. I had a few minutes before I needed to leave for the airport and was happy to give him the time he had requested. I'm glad I did.

The stoic, older gentleman related that he was a leader at the church and had attended the pastor's conference the week before where I had spoken on the subject of forgiveness. He went on to say that he had suffered a terrible wrong in his life in 1966 and for the past 50 years had been unable, even unwilling, to forgive those involved in causing him so much pain.

He admitted that his spiritual life was not what he wanted it to be even though he had studied the Bible and attended church regularly for decades. It was apparent that this was confusing and, at the same time, troubling to him. Why was he not maturing in his life before God?

He recognized that he had received forgiveness from the eternal penalty of sin the moment he placed his faith in Christ. Further, he was extremely grateful to know that he could obtain forgiveness for the sins he had committed after salvation by confessing them to God. But he could never bring himself to forgive those who had so grievously wronged him. And he knew that somehow that was holding him back.

Then, as tears filled his eyes, he joyfully announced that, after coming to a fuller understanding of what the Scriptures say about receiving and giving forgiveness, he was finally able to forgive as he had been forgiven. He said he immediately felt a tremendous burden had been lifted off of his shoulders and for the first time in 50 years felt true contentment.

Forgiveness did not mean that my new friend no longer considered what had happened to be bad. He was not excusing the horrible things that had been done to his family. He was not calling something wrong, right. Rather, he recognized the sin against him and his family and pardoned those who had done the evil. He no longer held hatred in his soul toward them. He no longer felt resentment or anger.

Later that day as I boarded my plane for the flight home I wondered how many Christians have sabotaged their own spiritual growth because they had missed or forgotten the critical truth that we are to forgive as we have been forgiven. So many of us hold on to resentment not realizing that it is toxic to our own spiritual health.

To fully appreciate the command to forgive others we must first recognize the depth of the sin problem that came as a result of the original disobedience of Adam as well as the subsequent acts of sin common to each of us. When we are totally aware of both the magnitude of the sin problem and the price paid by Jesus in love to solve that problem our motivation and enthusiasm for forgiving each other will increase. That is where we will begin in Chapters 1-3.

Chapter 4 will explore the death Christ died to pay the penalty of sin. Chapter 5 considers the individual's responsibility to place their faith in Jesus to forgive their sins and give them eternal life.

Chapters 6-8 deal with the consequences of post-salvation sinning and the one condition placed by God on the believer for the forgiveness of those sins. We will see that the sins we commit after salvation do not result in our being condemned once again but do cause the believer to lose that close intimate experiential relationship we were designed to have with God. This is what David calls the "joy of Thy salvation" in Psalm 51. This "fellowship" relationship can be restored only by an open and honest admission to God that what we did was wrong.

Chapters 9-10 address the responsibility of the believer to forgive others as we have been forgiven. We will note that this is not an optional aspect of the Christian life but a command from God. These chapters also stress that a refusal to forgive others after God has forgiven us is itself a sin and can cause much harm to our own spiritual walk.

My African friend squandered years of potential spiritual growth by his refusal to forgive. It is my sincere prayer that as you read this book you will be motivated not only to believe in Christ and receive forgiveness from the eternal penalty of sin, but also to confess post-salvation sins to God so that your time spent away from His fellowship will be minimal. And, ultimately, having an understanding and appreciation of those two truths, to *forgive others as we have been forgiven.*

The Choice

It all started with a choice, a bad choice.

❖ ❖ ❖

"According to most philosophers, God in making the world enslaved it. According to Christianity, in making it, He set it free. God had written, not so much a poem, but rather a play; a play he had planned as perfect, but which had necessarily been left to human actors and stage-managers, who had since made a great mess of it."

G.K Chesterton, Orthodoxy

❖ ❖ ❖

In the beginning, God gifted humanity with the ability to choose to submit to the Creator and love Him or refuse to submit and rebel against Him. But along with the ability to make free will moral decisions also came responsibility and consequences. God would hold the first couple accountable for the choices they made.

Like the original couple, we too have free will. We don't have *unlimited* free will, of course. I cannot will myself to become a giraffe, or to pole vault 35 feet. I cannot simply choose to defy gravity. If I jump out of an airplane at 10,000 feet without a parachute, the landing is going to be a bit abrupt. We all recognize the limitations of the will, but it is foolish to deny its existence.

Our will has limits and the boundaries of our volition are a part of God's sovereign choice. In creating us, God chose to make us choose. God's sovereignty does not force our choices for by definition, forced choices are not really choices. God has given us free will within a particular context. And in that context we have the ability, even the responsibility, to make literally hundreds of choices every day.

Not every choice we make has a moral component. Some of our decisions in life are morally neutral. It is unlikely that the choice of a dinner entrée or the color of our socks constitutes a free will moral decision. On the other hand, many decisions we make are a choice between something that is either clearly right or clearly wrong. In this case God holds us accountable for our decisions.

In the creation event God was not threatened in the least to give mankind the ability to choose whether to love and obey Him or to reject His love and disobey. The God revealed in the Bible places human beings in a position to freely accept Him or reject Him. He does not force love. We benefit from loving and obeying Him. God is perfectly content either way. He prefers to bless obedience. His desire is for us to love Him and He rewards loyalty. But God will hold us accountable for disobedience.

THE FIRST TEMPTATION

The preeminent Old Testament scholar Walter C. Kaiser Jr. taught,

> In order to have a good understanding of the New Testament one needs to have a competent grasp of the Old Testament. And in order to fully appreciate the Old Testament one would need to be thoroughly familiar with the message of the book of Genesis. And in order to comprehend the message of Genesis one must understand the significance of what is recorded in Genesis 1-3.[1]

The record of the temptation and fall of the first couple is fundamental to appreciating the message of the Bible as a whole and to understanding and appreciating the concept of forgiveness.

The Scriptures reveal the glory of God as He deals with His creation and its primary theme is the redemption of mankind through the sacrificial death of Jesus.[2] That narrative makes little sense if we fail to comprehend the magnitude of the problem of sin and its consequences.

When the Man and the Woman chose to defy God and rejected His plan, the results were negative beyond description. God had created something beautiful. And as Chesterton wrote, the Man and Woman "made a great mess of it." The account of this original rebellion is found in Genesis 3. If we are to appreciate the beauty of forgiveness we must first understand how God's perfect creation, something He proclaimed "very good," became something really "messed up."

Adam and Eve, our original parents, were placed in an environment that was perfect in every way, designed just for them. They were in communion with God, nature and themselves. They were beautiful people. Both the Man and Woman were highly intelligent. They had perfect health, perfect energy, perfect bodies and, well, perfect *everything*. Then one day in an act that can only be described as irrational, they said in effect, "That's not good enough."

From the moment Adam and Eve were created Satan had been looking for an opportunity to tempt the first couple to use their freedom to choose to turn away from God, to reject the Creator and His love. One would think that this temptation would prove futile. After all, what more could they want? Why would any rational being rebel against God's goodness? It is unthinkable but that is exactly what happened.

As Genesis Chapter 3 opens it is impossible to tell just how long the Man and the Woman had been in the Garden.[3] The text of Genesis gives no reason why the Fall of Man could not have happened on the eighth day.

As Genesis 2 concludes the creative act is complete. God had declared His creation *very good.* The Man and Woman occupied the Garden of Eden in perfection and the text tells us they were "naked and not ashamed" (Genesis 2:25). There was a certain innocence in the Garden that was what we would expect from the original couple. At this point they had no experience with evil. There was no need for clothing as only two humans existed and they were in perfect fellowship with God and each other.

However, there was another player on the scene and his description in Genesis 3:1 stands in stark contrast to the innocence of the man and woman. The serpent is described as "more crafty than any beast of the field." While it is not stated in Genesis 3, Revelation 12:9 confirms that the serpent is actually Satan.

The first sentence of Genesis 3 gives the careful reader a sense that something very negative is about to happen. It reminds me of a movie I once saw where the camera followed an unsuspecting young mother entering her home with a bag of groceries under each arm and then turned to show a menacing looking young man in a hood hiding behind the door with a butcher knife in his hand. At this point the soundtrack to the film took on an ominous tone, giving us the clue that this was probably not going to turn out well. And that's the feeling we get when we compare the ending of Genesis 2 and the beginning of Genesis 3. Something really bad is about to take place.

The Serpent began his interaction with the Woman with what looks on the surface to be a relatively innocent question, "Indeed has God said, 'You shall not eat from any tree of the Garden?'" In what the German pastor Dietrich Bonhoeffer called "the first conversation about God," Satan immediately distorts the *truth* about God. In reality that is *not* what God had said.

At this point, it would be helpful to see this from the Woman's perspective. In her mind the Serpent posed no threat. She sensed no reason to be on alert. But she was badly mistaken. The Serpent was a danger and it was serious. He was devious and manipulative, the polar opposite of the Woman.

SATAN IS A MASTER OF THE COUNTERFEIT

Satan rarely tempts directly. His attacks are normally oblique. His temptations commonly come in the form of disguise. He uses his intelligence and craftiness to knock us off balance and divert our attention away from our Creator and onto something else. It is then that we become vulnerable to failure.

Satan, in a sly way, challenged the goodness of God. When he opens a dialogue with the Woman, the Serpent employs an interesting rhetorical ploy. He says, in effect, "Help me out here. I am having trouble understanding this. Did God *really* say you weren't to eat from any tree of the Garden? Seriously?" He follows by challenging the goodness of God and implying that God is afraid that they might become as smart as He is if they eat from the forbidden tree. It's incredibly under-handed but a shrewd starting point to engage the Woman in conversation.

Again, observe carefully the contrast: the Man and Woman in openness and innocence and the Serpent in craftiness. I am not making excuses for the Woman here. I am simply setting the context. To be fair, the Woman was up against a formidable opponent; one few of us will ever have to face directly.

Our original parents were not familiar with sin and evil. If we were to transfer them to today's context we might say they were not "street smart." Satan, on the other hand, was the very essence of evil.

Satan's approach to Eve was much like something that happened in my hometown of Houston a number of years ago. A good looking, well dressed thirty-five year old man knocked on the door of a number of homes during the midday heat of a Houston summer in 1990 claiming that his car had broken down and asked if he could use the phone to call a wrecker to rescue him. Several women felt sorry for him and, sensing no threat, invited him into their homes only to be brutally sexually assaulted by the man. The women trusted the man because they felt no danger. But it ended up tragically for them.

Sometime before this, how long before we cannot say with certainty, but probably a significant period of time before, Satan rebelled against the same God that created us, the same God we worship: an infinitely holy, good, righteous, fair, just and loving God. For reasons not re-vealed, Satan concluded he could be "like God" and even overturn God's sovereignty over the universe.

> "How you have fallen from heaven,
> O star of the morning, son of the dawn!
> You have been cut down to the earth,
> You who have weakened the nations!
>
> "But you said in your heart,
> 'I will ascend to heaven;
> I will raise my throne above the stars of God,
> And I will sit on the mount of assembly
>
> In the recesses of the north.
> 'I will ascend above the heights of the clouds;
> I will make myself like the Most High'"
> (Isaiah 14:12-14).

How could a highly intelligent creature ever reason that he could overthrow the Supreme Creator? It is surely irrational. But it happened. Then again, we practice that same kind of irrationality on a regular basis when we know what God expects of us and we reject it. We know what the God ordained boundaries on behavior are; yet we rebel anyway. It's the same absurdity.

Satan's original sin was pride. Pride clouds clear thinking and motivates bad decisions. All sin is, in some way, related to pride.

In the Woman's response to the Serpent it becomes clear that the precision of the Word of the Lord had not been retained. This was a huge mistake on the woman's part then, and it is a huge mistake when it happens now.

The Woman said to the Serpent,

> "From the fruit of the trees of the garden we may eat; but from the fruit of the tree which is in the middle of the garden, God has said, 'You shall not eat from it or touch it, or you will die'" (Genesis 3:2-3).

There are some areas in life where being naïve can be refreshing. But there are other areas where naïveté can be very dangerous. Taking God's Word casually is one of them. We are called upon to "correctly handle" the Word of Truth (2 Timothy 2:15), which means we must carefully observe what the text says, then properly interpret it, and finally, thoughtfully apply it. This can easily be remembered by, "what does it say, what does it mean, what am I to do?"

God's Word is His self disclosure to man. Therefore, it demands our highest attention. If engineers and doctors practiced their trade the same way some people do Bible study we would have bridges collapsing and patients dying in considerable numbers. State Licensing Boards would pull licenses to practice for such incompetence. In an even greater way, the Word of God demands precision. He has spoken. May we never handle it in a sloppy manner.

So what did God actually tell the Man about the one prohibition in the Garden?

> And the Lord God commanded the man saying, "From any tree of the Garden you may eat freely; but from the tree of the knowledge of good and evil you shall not eat, for in the day you eat from it you shall surely die" (Genesis 2:16-17).

In her answer to the serpent, the woman expresses three areas of imprecision. Were the three a result of her husband not properly relaying the information to her, or because Adam gave her the information accurately but she did not listen carefully? I suspect that given the environment of the Garden and the perfection of the original couple, he gave it accurately and she was listening carefully. The problem came when she was thrown off guard by the craftiness of the serpent. Nevertheless there are three areas where she gets it wrong.

First, she minimized the provision of the Lord. The Lord had said, "You may freely eat" but Eve simply said, "We may eat." Second, she added to the prohibition. The Lord had said nothing about touching the tree, but she misquoted God saying, "Neither shall you touch it". Third, she weakened the penalty for sin. God had declared, "You shall surely die." (Hebrew: *mot tamut)* but Eve simply said, "lest you die." (A weakened form of the phrase.)

These are not trivial distortions. When Satan saw that the woman had not retained precision of God's prohibition, he immediately responded, "You surely shall not die!"

It is interesting that Satan's words were closer to the original decree than were Eve's. If she had been thinking, this should have been a big red flag. The serpent was not an ignorant beast. He did not need "just a little help" understanding what God had said. This was a trap. She should have ended the conversation right there and walked away. But she didn't.

In verse 5 the Serpent maligns God's motivation. He said,

> "For God knows that in the day you eat from it
> your eyes will be opened, and you will be like God,
> knowing good and evil" (Genesis 3:5).

Satan's charge is fundamentally this: "God does not have your best interest in mind. He is holding you back from becoming all you can be. He cares nothing about you. God is not essentially good." That's it. That's the satanic lie. He spoke it in the Garden and he has been repeating it to generation after generation. It is nothing less than a challenge to the integrity of God and to His infinite perfection.

Isn't it ironic that Satan would bring up being "like God"? That was *his* original sin. He wanted the position of God for himself. Now he challenges the woman to desire the same thing, for to be " like God knowing good and evil" is a temptation to self-deification, becoming master over our own lives. Victor P. Hamilton in his commentary on Genesis put it well, "Deification is a fantasy difficult to repress and hard to reject."[4]

THE FIRST FREE WILL MORAL DECISION

It didn't take long for the temptation to achieve its goal. What theologians call "The Fall" is recorded in rapid succession with a sequence of verbs: she saw, she took, she ate, she gave, he ate" (Genesis 3:6).

The text of Genesis devotes more time to the dialogue and the tension of the event than the actual submission to temptation. This shows how temptation to sin often works in our own lives.

When we fall prey to the lure of sin it frequently happens really fast. One day we are walking along life's road minding our own business and then, for just a moment, we pause and flirt with sin. Rather than perceive it as something to be avoided at all costs, we view it as a clear, cool mountain stream.

It looks so inviting and we just want to stick our foot in and enjoy the feeling of the water rushing across our skin. The next instant we find ourselves swept away and wondering, "What just happened?" Our perception of the stream was faulty. Rather than being refreshing it was devastatingly destructive.

Genesis 3:7 records the aftermath of the first sin. Their "eyes were opened" and they knew they were naked. They now viewed their nakedness as a problem and moved to provide a solution to the problem. They sewed fig leaves into garments to cover their bodies.

The noted Old Testament scholar Allen Ross comments,

> The results, of course, were anticlimactic. Their eyes were opened, but the promise of divine enlightenment did not come about. What was right before was now very wrong. They knew more, but the additional knowledge was evil. Mistrust and alienation replaced the security and intimacy they had enjoyed.[5]

Man used his will to rebel against his Creator rather than to worship and love Him. While in one sense the results were, as Ross put it, anticlimactic, on a larger scale they were devastating. Sin entered into a creation that was very good. Because man used his free will to reject God, a great divide came to exist between creature and Creator. That which God designed as perfect was now polluted by the rebellion of man.

Chapter 1 Summary

■ God created the man and woman in perfection and gave them free will.

■ Their will was not unlimited but existed within the boundaries of God's sovereign choice.

■ The original couple used their will to rebel against God rather than to love and worship Him.

■ The results of this rebellion were devastating.

Something to Consider

When faced with temptation we should remember that Satan rarely tempts us straight on. He was crafty in the beginning and he remains crafty today. His temptations are designed to catch us off balance and often in ways where we think we could never fail. He uses our perceived self-sufficiency and self-confidence against us. We must be ever diligent to keep our focus in life on our perfect Creator, remembering that He is ultimately good and has our best interest in mind. He wants our success. He deeply desires to bless us.

2

The Consequences of Rebellion

The choice to sin is no small thing.

❖ ❖ ❖

For the wages of sin is death but, the free gift of God is eternal
life in Christ Jesus our Lord.

The Apostle Paul, Romans 6:23

Man has always been his own most vexing problem.

Richard Neihbor

❖ ❖ ❖

Rebellion against God is never wise. It carries with it a serious cost. God loved Adam and Eve before their rebellion and afterward. But His love did not cancel the fact that He had promised sure death for disobedience. God is love, but He is also righteous and just.

Adam and Eve had been told that there would be consequences to disobedience and they would be severe. "On the day you eat from it [the Tree of the Knowledge of Good and Evil] you shall surely die" (Genesis 2:17). The Hebrew phrase *mot tamut* translated into English means "you will absolutely die."

It is important to note that the man and woman knew nothing of death before their disobedience. They had never observed it. Everything in their environment was alive and prospering. The couple knew only life, not the cessation of it. But the moment they took the fruit and ate, death entered the world.

Adam and Eve did not immediately die physically when they sinned, but the *process* of physical death began. We learn from Genesis 5 that Adam was 930 years old when he died physically. We are never told Eve's age at her death. Because of their disobedience, physical death entered into a perfect world. But it was never meant to be that way. That is why human beings grieve at the death of loved ones. Even believers in Jesus Christ, who know their believing beloved is in Heaven in a place of no more pain, no more tears, no more death, we still grieve. We do not grieve as those who have no hope, but we grieve nonetheless. Death was not designed to be the norm.

However, there is more to the aspect of death than just physical death. At the moment Adam and Eve rebelled against God there came to be an alienation or separation between them and their Creator. They had a relationship with God but it was no longer a relationship of blessing. They were now associated in a negative way rather than in a positive one. They were separated from the blessing of God. The man and woman each stood condemned before Him. There remained a relationship between creature and Creator but it was now a negative one.

The outcome of rebellion was both physical death and what theologians have called "spiritual death." The couple died spiritually the instant they disobeyed. The process of physical death, which began immediately, was completed some time later.

Further, because of the original rebellion, all of creation suffered. The ground, which was once perfectly fertile, would now produce "thorns and thistles." Animals would die and suffer hardship. Paul describes creation as "groaning and suffering pains of childbirth" because of original disobedience (Romans 8:22).

God created a perfect world with perfect environment. Adam had been placed in charge of all of the earth and the consequences of his failure overflowed into the entirety of his area of responsibility. When a leader fails, very often those under his leadership suffer. In this case, Adam was given charge over all the earth. Because he failed, all the earth suffers along with mankind.

Although Eve sinned first, it is Adam's sin for which God holds us all accountable. The New Testament explains that Eve was deceived but Adam was not (1 Timothy 2:14).

Therefore, it is Adam's sin that is passed down to the human race. It is Adam's sin that causes us to be born in a state that theologians call total depravity. There are competing views as to the specifics of just how this occurs, of how we could be born under condemnation for something someone else did. But Paul is clear in his letter to the Romans that this is the case.

> Therefore, just as through one man sin entered into the world, and death through sin, and so death spread to all men because all sinned— [when Adam sinned] (Romans 5:12).

TOTAL DEPRAVITY

Given the wonder and preciousness of a newborn baby, the idea of being born under condemnation or totally depraved deserves some explanation. Depravity is such a strong word. The English word means, "morally corrupt, wicked, perverted, deviant, degenerate." When I think of depravity I generally think of child pornographers, sexually abusive parents, rapists or the three men that murdered my friend Miguel Gomez.

Miguel was my workout partner in the late 80's. He was a black belt in Tae Kwon Do as well as a champion Golden Gloves boxer. The days I sparred with Miguel I knew I had better bring my best or I would get hurt. When I first met Miguel he was a cheerful 25-year-old recent immigrant from Puerto Rico. He was an honest, humble, hard working young man who was willing to clean tables at a restaurant to earn a living. I vividly remember how excited he was when he announced to us one morning that he and his wife were going to have a baby. His joy was overwhelming. And we were happy for him. Miguel's primary concern was that he was barely getting by financially at the time and he had no idea how he was going to pay for the new baby.

About two weeks before his daughter was born Miguel announced that he had taken a second job as a clerk at a convenience store, working the late night/early morning shift. All of his friends, myself included, urged him to reconsider. This was a dangerous job in a dangerous part of the city and the pay was so meager that it hardly seemed worth it. I even offered give him whatever he was going to make at that job until he could find something safer. After all, he was going to be a father and his child would need him. But Miguel would not accept the money. He told me his pride would not allow it.

Just three days after his daughter was born, at 3:00 AM on a Friday morning, Miguel noticed three men playing with a gun in the parking lot right in front of the store. Instead of calling the police he went out and asked the men to put the gun away. They assured him that they would. But as Miguel turned and re-entered the store one of the men used the gun to shoot him in the back. Miguel fell to his knees, unable to move. The man then circled around to the front of my friend, put the gun right between his eyes and pulled the trigger. His wife was now without her husband. His daughter would never know her father.

That's what I think of when I think of depravity. I certainly don't think of myself. Sure, I have done things, said things, and thought things that I regret. But God would not consider me depraved, would He? Isn't that term reserved for the really evil people, the really bad people? The Bible says, "not so fast," we are *all* depraved.

This is a serious issue, one foundational to our spiritual growth, for if we do not understand total depravity, we will never understand grace. And if we do not understand grace we will not understand forgiveness and if we don't understand forgiveness we will never grow to a place of maturity with respect to our relationship with our Creator.

MADE IN THE IMAGE OF GOD

Genesis 1:26-27 relates that mankind, both male and female, were made in the image of God. This was not said of any other part or aspect of God's creation. In some respects, man resembles God. It does not mean that man has become God or that God created "little gods," but rather man resembles God. The Protestant Reformers regarded the "image of God" in man as referring to man's immaterial nature as created for rational, moral, and spiritual fellowship with God.

Man has intellect, emotion and will, all aspects of what we might call personality. In addition man has the ability to reason and the capacity to make moral decisions. Man is not merely conscious but has self-consciousness. God, too, possesses these qualities. God thinks. God feels. And God chooses, or acts.

We readily acknowledge that while God thinks, feels and acts with perfection, our thinking, expression of emotion and choices fall far short of perfection. I would deny a perfect correspondence between our emotion, for example, and God's emotion. It is a mistake to take the concept of human emotion, as it is, and impose that back upon God. But God's emotion is not so totally unlike ours that there is *no* correspondence. If there is no correspondence at all, then what is revealed in the Bible makes no sense and there would be no revelation. We understand God's emotion, for example, to be *in some way* like ours and therefore we can know something of God.

Because of Adam's sin, we are all born condemned. He represented us in making that decision. We might complain that this is unfair and that we would have chosen differently had we been in Adam's place, but who are we kidding? We have sinned more times than we could count, *after* receiving a new nature as a Christian. You and I would have done the same thing Adam did. We may have sinned sooner. We may have held out longer. But we would have done the same thing. We have proven that over and over. We have no basis for complaint.

After Adam sinned he was totally incapable of saving himself. And so are we. If he were to be made right with God, God had to make the first move. And that is just what He did. Adam and Eve hid; God sought after the man and woman. His pursuit of them is undeserved favor. This is grace. This is critical. This is foundational to everything else in theology. This is foundational to our spiritual lives.

THE IMAGE OF GOD IN HUMANS IS SEVERELY DAMAGED BUT NOT ELIMINATED

Even in our fallen state, human beings retain the image of God. His image in man is severely damaged but not destroyed by sin. It is for this reason that we are forbidden to murder anyone, whether saved or unsaved:

> "Whoever sheds the blood of man, by man shall his blood be shed; for in the image of God has God made man" (Genesis 9:6).

If unsaved persons do not retain something of the image of God, the reasoning behind this prohibition (against murdering them) would make no sense. We are not to murder because, among other things, our fellow man is a special aspect of God's creation, made in His image.

Likewise, we are told not to curse other human beings, since they are in God's image, and hence we would be effectively cursing God,

> "With the tongue we praise our Lord and Father, and with it we curse men, who have been made in God's likeness. Out of the same mouth come praise and cursing. My brothers, this should not be" (James 3:8–10).

In brief, sin severely *damages* but does not *completely erase* the image of God in human beings; God's image in man is *marred* but not *eliminated*. Even the most evil of human beings retain some resemblance of God's likeness.

Since the whole person is made in God's image, and since sin affects the whole person, the first thing to be said is that the effect of sin on God's image in fallen human beings extends to every dimension of our being—emotion, intellect and will.

Sin penetrates and permeates our whole being. Humans are born *completely*, not partially, depraved; that is, every aspect of our being is affected by sin. No element of human nature is unaffected by inherited sin, even though no aspect is completely destroyed by it.

It is in this sense that sinful humanity is appropriately described as "totally depraved." This *does not* mean that fallen humans are as sinful as they could be, but it *does* mean that apart from Christ we are not as good as we should be (in accordance with God's perfect nature).

Adam and Eve could still think, feel, and choose; they did not, because of sin, lose these qualities of personhood. If they had, they would no longer be persons. They were able to converse with and understand God after their sin. They were still human, and therefore they retained the image of God, even though they were *fallen* humans, consequently incapable of either initiating or attaining their own salvation.[6]

And that is the point of this chapter. After the rebellion, after the Fall, Adam and Eve were completely helpless. They were separated from the blessing of God and they had begun the process of physical death. If the original couple were to have any chance at deliverance from their predicament at all, God had to intervene, and, in love, He did. His intervention, His offer to them of undeserved favor, is called grace.

Chapter 2 Summary

■ Rebellion against God carried with it serious consequences. "For the wages of sin is death but the gift of God is eternal life through Christ Jesus our Lord" (Romans 6:23).

■ At the instant the man and woman disobeyed they died spiritually, meaning that there was now an alienation or separation between the couple and God. They were still in a relationship with Him but it was now a negative rather than a positive one.

■ When they disobeyed, physical death was introduced into the world.

■ Total depravity does not mean that man is as sinful as he could be, but rather that apart from Christ we are not as good as we must be.

Something to Consider

So many people today recognize that something is not right with their lives and want very much to have a positive relationship with God. They do what they can to clean up their lives and attempt to make themselves acceptable to God. However, restoration to a right relationship with God cannot be accomplished on our own. We need God. One who is totally depraved cannot present themselves to God and be found acceptable no matter how much they change their behavior. This is where the grace of God comes in.

Grace

❖ ❖ ❖

Through false emphasis by many religious leaders, Christianity has become in the estimation of a large part of the public, no more than an ethical system. The revealed fact, however, is that the supreme feature of the Christian faith is that supernatural, saving, transforming work of God, which is made possible through the infinite sacrifice of Christ and which, in sovereign grace, is freely bestowed on all who believe.

L.S. Chafer

❖ ❖ ❖

On October 16, 1987 Scott Shaw snapped the photograph that would win him the Pulitzer Prize for spot news photography. It was of a soiled and bloodied 18-month-old little girl being pulled from a well into which she had fallen two days before.

I remember like it was yesterday the frequent news updates of Baby Jessica's fall 22 feet down that 8 inch pipe and the rescue efforts that captured the hearts of just about everyone. President Reagan said afterward, "everybody in America became godmothers and godfathers of Jessica while this was going on." It took rescue workers 58 hours to pull that little girl out of a hole that she could have never climbed out of on her own.

Jessica McClure is now an adult and has two children of her own. She remembers nothing of the episode. She still lives in Midland, Texas, just a short distance from the infamous well, now capped. Aside from losing a toe to amputation Jessica seems to have suffered no long term problems as a result of the ordeal. But she knows that she is alive today due to the extraordinary efforts of those rescue workers. It was all because of them. She was truly helpless. There was no way she could have rescued herself from that situation.

When Adam and Eve rebelled against God they put themselves in a hole that was far deeper and far more serious than the one that trapped Baby Jessica. More serious, because had Jessica died in that pipe she would have gone immediately to Heaven. The finished work of Christ would have been applied to her account by God because, as a baby, she had no possibility of fulfilling the one condition necessary for the receiving of eternal life: faith.[7] Had Adam and Eve suffered physical death right after their fall, they would not have gone to Heaven but to eternal judgment.

At this point, we are faced with this question: How does a loving, holy and sovereign God respond to the disobedience of His creation? Will He leave the Man and Woman in "just" condemnation? He would be justified in doing so; after all, they had disobeyed. Will He eliminate the Man and Woman altogether and start over? Or, will He look the other way as if nothing had happened and hope that they obey next time?

No, God will not, in fact *cannot,* just simply look the other way and hope that man is faithful in the future. Holiness will not allow that. But God does not eliminate the Man and the Woman either. We might have expected that outcome given the warning, "on the day you eat from it you will surely die." That sounds clear enough. As I mentioned previously, *mot tamut* should be understood, "you will definitely die." There is no ambivalence here, "you disobey and you are definitely going to die." But just when it looks the worst for the original couple, just as it appears that all hope is gone, grace is introduced. God will provide a way out.

Grace is unmerited favor. It is something we neither earn nor deserve. If we earned it, it would not be grace. The acronym, GRACE works well: *God's Riches At Christ's Expense.*

Grace is the basis upon which we were delivered from the "hole" we found ourselves in. It is *free* to us, but it cost God a great deal. (This will be the subject of Chapter 4.) Christ's sacrifice made grace possible. Without it there could be no rescue. Without grace we would have been left in condemnation. I cannot say this emphatically enough: we must comprehend and appreciate grace if we are ever to move forward in the Christian life.

The reaction of Adam and Eve to their sin is instructive: They do not seek out God and acknowledge their guilt. In fact, we observe quite the opposite. They attempt to hide from God and when confronted, attempt to make excuses.

> They heard the sound of the Lord God walking in the garden in the cool of the day, and the man and his wife hid themselves from the presence of the Lord God among the trees of the garden. Then the Lord God called to the man, and said to him, "Where are you?" He said, "I heard the sound of You in the garden, and I was afraid because I was naked; so I hid myself." And He said, "Who told you that you were naked? Have you eaten from the tree of which I commanded you not to eat?" The man said, "The woman whom You gave *to be* with me, she gave me from the tree, and I ate." Then the Lord God said to the woman, "What is this you have done?" And the woman said, "The serpent deceived me, and I ate" (Genesis 3:8-13).

Notice that it is God who seeks the couple, not the couple that seek God. When God calls out, "Where are you?" and asks, "Who told you that you were naked?" it is not a request for information. God is omniscient, meaning He knows everything. Rather, it is an opportunity for man to come clean with his Creator.

When confronted with a direct question as to their eating of the forbidden fruit, Adam's first instinct is to make excuses, even blaming God in the process. "This woman who you gave me…" Adam's instinct was to blame someone else for his own rebellion. And that instinct to shift blame is still in our DNA today. Adam blames the Woman and God. Eve blames the Serpent and makes the excuse that she was deceived, but both eventually acknowledge their rebellious disobedience.

Before God would introduce the solution, the couple had to openly admit they had a problem. They had used their will to rebel against God rather than obey Him. They violated His holiness and that is no small thing. For, that which is profane cannot have intimacy with that which is holy.

Once they admitted their guilt, God presented the solution. Interestingly, the resolution comes in the midst of what are called "the oracles of the Fall," or the Curse as it is commonly known. It is essential to understand the Curse before we will be in a position to fully appreciate the gracious solution.

The "Curse" includes the idea of "banishment from the place of blessing." All of creation would be banished from the place of blessing, fertility and harmony. There will now be a perpetual conflict between good and evil, between those who follow God and those who reject Him.

When someone dies without having placed their faith in the person and work of Jesus Christ they are not annihilated, they do not cease to exist. No, rather they forever remain as they are, apart from the blessing of God. They were born separated from God's blessing; they will remain that way eternally.

THE ORACLES OF THE FALL

The oracle against the woman deals with childbirth and the other with her relationship to the man.

> To the woman He said,
> "I will greatly multiply
> Your pain in childbirth,
> In pain you will bring forth children;
> Yet your desire will be for your husband,
> And he will rule over you"(Genesis 3:16).

First, the process of bringing a child into the world will be painful. Second, the man, in his fallen state, will seek to dominate the woman.

The second of these two requires a bit more explanation.[8] The passage is asserting that the woman in her fallen state will have a tendency to attempt to dominate her husband, and at the same time, the husband will be inclined to dominate the wife. The point being that what was going to be comfortable and pleasant, will now be a constant struggle because of the rebellion. God is not saying it *should* be this way, He is saying because of the rebellion, it *will* be this way. The effects of the Fall may be softened when believers are walking in fellowship with God, but the effects of the Fall will continue to be a reality until the day we die.

As for the man, work, which was designed to be natural and trouble free, would now be painful and difficult.

Then to Adam He said, "Because you have listened
to the voice of your wife, and have eaten from the
tree about which I commanded you, saying, 'You
shall not eat from it';

Cursed is the ground because of you;
In toil you will eat of it
All the days of your life.
"Both thorns and thistles it shall grow for you;
And you will eat the plants of the field;
By the sweat of your face
You will eat bread,
Till you return to the ground,
Because from it you were taken;
For you are dust,
And to dust you shall return" (Genesis 3:17-19).

The oracle against the Serpent is found in Genesis 3:15. This verse is understood by serious students of the Word of God as the first mention of the gospel in the Bible. It is the John 3:16 of Genesis although admittedly it does not read that way at first glance.

The Lord God said to the serpent,
"Because you have done this,
Cursed are you more than all cattle,
And more than every beast of the field;
On your belly you will go,
And dust you will eat
All the days of your life;
And I will put enmity
Between you and the woman,
And between your seed and her seed;
He shall bruise you on the head,
And you shall bruise him on the heel. (Genesis 3:14-15).

The "Seed of the Woman" includes, in the broadest sense, all of humanity. But the ultimate fulfillment of the Seed of the Woman is Jesus Christ.

The Seed of the Serpent is a bit more difficult to identify but it likely includes all who reject the Lord and side with Satan against God. The Seed of the Serpent will injure the Seed of the Woman but in the end the Seed of the Woman will crush the head of the Seed of the Serpent. This found its completion at the Crucifixion of Jesus.

Those who were evil inflicted pain upon our Lord during the ordeal of His arrest, trials and crucifixion. They *injured* Him. They did not *conquer* Him. They did not crush Him. In like manner, our rebellion injured Him. It was our rebellion, our evil that brought about the necessity of the Cross.

Genesis 3:15 signals God's willingness to provide a way out of the dilemma caused by the rebellion of our original parents. They deserved death, as do those who follow them in disobedience. And that includes us all. We have all rebelled against God. We have all fallen short of His glory. God, in grace, would sacrifice the Seed of the Woman (Jesus) to pay the penalty due to Adam and Eve, as well as to you and me.

GRACE AND WORKS

As stated above, grace is unmerited favor. It is neither earned nor deserved. It is not a payment rendered for anything we have done. It is not something we can ever repay.

In the fourth chapter of Romans, Paul illustrates the concept of justification by grace through faith by using Abraham, a familiar figure from Jewish history. Abraham was, and is, greatly respected as a righteous man by all three of the major monotheistic faiths, Christianity, Judaism and Islam. He was arguably the greatest man of faith of his age. But he did not *earn* God's favor.

> What then shall we say that Abraham, our forefather according to the flesh, has found? For if Abraham was justified by works, he has something to boast about, but not before God. For what does the Scripture say? "Abraham believed God, and it was credited to him as righteousness." Now to the one who works, his wage is not credited as a favor {Greek, *charis*, grace, favor, gift} but as what is due. But to the one who does not work, but believes in Him who justifies the ungodly, his faith is credited as righteousness (Romans 4:1-5).

Suppose for a moment that you work 40 hours a week for an employer and do a really good job. You show up on time for work, follow company policy, cooperate with your fellow workers and put great effort into everything you do. Then when payday comes the boss calls you into the office and says, "I have decided to be gracious to you and pay you for this week's work." I suspect you would be somewhat surprised. You might think that it was gracious of the boss to give you a job or to provide a good working environment, but to pay you for the work done? That would not be a gracious thing; it would be the *expected* thing. I work for you, you compensate me. It is an exchange of services for pay.

Grace is undeserved favor ...
Grace is a gift from God

But suppose you were not able to work that week and you had no vacation time coming, no sick days accrued or personal days accumulated. Perhaps you were ill, or you had a family member who needed your help or any other of a dozen reasons why you might legitimately not be able to work that week. And then the boss calls you in and says, "Even though you were unable to work, I'm going to be gracious to you and pay you for this week." Your attitude would be quite different. In the first case the worker deserved his wages. In the second case, he did not.

Grace is undeserved favor. We do not earn grace. We do not work for grace. Grace is a gift from God. If we work for it, it is by definition, no longer grace.

An understanding and appreciation of grace is necessary if one is to approach the subject of forgiveness with eyes that see. We were in a hole deeper than Baby Jessica and every bit as helpless to reverse the situation. She had to rely upon outside help. And so do we. Because we are totally unable to accomplish our own deliverance, God had to do it for us.

Grace was introduced. A solution was offered that was totally undeserved. The more I walk down life's road, the more I appreciate the grace and mercy of God. We needed it to be rescued from the eternal penalty of sin and we need it to exist every day on this earth.

Today in churches I see two different approaches when it comes to sin and grace. Some tend to look upon the Christian life as one of avoidance of sin and their preaching will inevitably reflect this position. Their sermons are marked by an exhortation to stop sinning. They often use guilt as the primary motivating tool in their messages neglecting almost totally the forgiveness and freedom God offers.

Others view the spiritual life as growing in grace and in the knowledge of our Lord and Savior Jesus Christ, learning to love God more each day and recognizing that the one who loves God will obey His commandments.

The former group is often accused of overemphasizing sin in their preaching and promoting legalism. The latter is sometimes accused of neglecting the preaching of sin and perhaps even promoting it.[9]

The issue is not one of preaching sin *or* grace but sin *and* grace. Both truths are relevant to our spiritual lives and our spiritual growth. If we are ever to recover from sin we must understand grace and if we are ever to understand grace and forgiveness we must understand sin, the seriousness of it, and where it came from.

Chapter 3 Summary

■ Grace is defined as unmerited favor.

■ Grace is necessary because, man in a state of condemnation and depravity, cannot accomplish his own rescue from sin.

■ An understanding and appreciation of grace is necessary if one is to approach the subject of forgiveness objectively.

Something to Consider

Most of us are uncomfortable receiving a gift. Our instinct is to resolve to do something for the person giving the gift in return. The ancient Greeks and Romans viewed gifts in that way. There was an implied reciprocity in the giving of any gift. "I give this to you, I expect something in return. Maybe not today, but someday."

However, when God gives a gift it is truly free. We cannot ever begin to pay God back, or "return the favor." God's grace, by definition, is free. When we come to more fully comprehend that truth, our lives will never be the same. The chains of guilt and self condemnation will fall off and perhaps for the first time, we will truly begin to live.

The High Cost of Rebellion:
The Death of Jesus Christ

❖ ❖ ❖

"No problem can be solved from the same level of consciousness that created it." *Albert Einstein*

"That the blood of Christ was shed to buy our souls from death and Hell is a wonder of compassion which fills the angels with amazement, and it ought to overwhelm us with adoring love whenever we think of it." *Charles Spurgeon*

"The gospel is like an illuminating radiance that lights up the landscape of reality, allowing us to see things as they really are." *Alister McGrath*

❖ ❖ ❖

I t is said that the well known British preacher of the 19th century Charles Spurgeon designed each of his sermons so that at some point they intersected with the Cross. I cannot verify that as a fact, but if it is true, I think Spurgeon was on to something.

The Crucifixion and Resurrection of Jesus was the central and defining event in all of human history. It is through the lens of the Cross that the rest of life comes into focus. And if we are to fully value the subject of forgiveness, we must fully value the price God paid to rescue us. God did not sacrifice some unknown angel who lived in some remote part of the universe who had no friends or family and would not be missed. He sacrificed that which was most dear to Him, His eternal Son. It could be said that in providing a solution to the sin problem, God held nothing back. He gave everything He had.

Adam and Eve created a problem that they could not solve on their own. The sin problem was simply too big. They were totally helpless to affect their own rescue. God had to make the first move and He did.

God did not have a problem. They did. The problem was fully theirs. But God freely chose to provide a way out for rebellious humanity, even though the only way out would be extremely costly to Him.

I seriously doubt that we will ever *fully* appreciate the suffering our Lord endured on our behalf until we take our last breath here on earth and breathe in that first breath of celestial air. In that moment when we see face to face the One who sacrificed everything so that we might stand on heavenly soil and enjoy fellowship with Him forever we will, perhaps for the first time, fully appreciate the death that Jesus died for us.

As we gaze upon those nail scared hands and feet I suspect that we will be overwhelmed with the depth of His sacrifice and the immensity of His love. In that instant what we have known since the moment we trusted Christ will be confirmed: we are not standing there because of any merit of our own but because of the love, righteousness and goodness of the One in whose presence we will then find ourselves.

Through the lens of the Cross
the rest of life comes into focus

He did it all. We appropriate the finished work of Christ on the Cross by grace through faith *apart from works*. We will not be able to look upon the memorial scars of His resurrection body and claim that we are there because of anything good in us.

As far as I can tell, Jesus has the only resurrection body with scars, and that makes perfect sense to me. His wounds will forever be a reminder to us of what it took for God to rescue us from the consequences of sin. As we live eternally in a place of perfection and ultimate bliss we will never forget why we are there.

> For God so loved the world, that He gave His only be-
> gotten Son that whosoever believeth in Him shall nev-
> er perish but have everlasting life (John 3:16).

THE ARREST OF THE MESSIAH

The most significant event in human history is the death and resurrection of Jesus Christ. I include both of these into one event because the two constitute a package deal. When outlining the gospel he preached, the apostle Paul wrote to the Corinthians,

> For I delivered to you as of first importance what I also received, that Christ died for our sins according to the Scriptures and that He was buried and that He was raised again on the third day, according to the Scriptures (1 Corinthians 15:3-4).

While we may not have a full appreciation of the Crucifixion and Resurrection of Jesus until we see Him in Eternity, it is certainly beneficial to spend time on this side of Heaven considering the event that is central to the reality of forgiveness.

Let's first consider the sequence of events leading up to the arrest of Jesus as we can recreate them from the gospel accounts:

1. The Sanhedrin, at the suggestion of the high priest, had determined to kill Jesus (Matt 26:3-4). (The Jewish leadership viewed Him as a threat to them both politically and religiously. Their solution: kill Him.)

2. Judas, one of Jesus' disciples, entered into an arrangement with the high priest to act as betrayer (Matt 26:14-15).

3. It was decided to postpone the execution until after the Passover season (Matt 26:5). Why? Like most self righteous religious people, they were, by nature, fearful. They were afraid of the possibility that the crowds in Jerusalem for the Passover would rise up against them after witnessing Jesus' very positive reception on Palm Sunday.

4. From that time on, Judas was continually watching for an opportunity to deliver Christ into the hands of the authorities (Matt 26:16).

5. During the Passover supper, Jesus revealed to Judas that He was aware of the arrangement he had made with the priests (Matt 26:25).

6. Judas rejects the offer of forgiveness that Jesus extended by offering him the piece of bread. Satan enters into Judas. Jesus tells Judas, "What

you are going to do, do quickly." Or to paraphrase, "I know it's you. What are you waiting for?" (John 13:27).

7. Judas, stunned, leaves the Upper Room and goes to the High Priest, who now decides to move forward with the arrest, as their informer has been "found out." A large group of soldiers and armed men is quickly rounded up. The participation of the Roman soldiers implies that Pilate had been previously consulted on the plans to arrest Jesus. Judas probably leads them first to the Upper Room, and not finding Jesus there, assumes He has gone to Gethsemane, where Judas knew they had planned to spend the night (John 18:1-3).[10]

At around 10 or 11 o'clock the night before the Crucifixion, Jesus and His disciples (minus Judas) made their way from the Upper Room across the Kidron Valley and to the Garden of Gethsemane. Incidentally, both the home in which they ate the Last Supper and the Garden of Gethsemane were likely owned by Mark's family. (The same Mark that wrote the gospel bearing his name.)

After arriving at the Garden, Jesus spent some time in intense prayer, praying repeatedly, "Father, if it be Thy will let this cup pass from Me. Nevertheless, not My will but Thy will be done" (Luke 22:42).

Sometime after midnight, just as Jesus finished praying, Judas arrived at the Garden with a large contingent of armed men. Their number and their weapons, "with swords and clubs," would suggest that, in their minds the man they intended to take into custody was a serious, maybe even a dangerous, criminal. Perhaps they feared that the eleven remaining disciples would defend their Master at any cost.

It is important to recognize, that throughout this entire process, Jesus is in complete control. The Father made it clear to the Son in the Garden (in some way not recorded) that this was the path that He was to take. There was no other way to provide for man's salvation. In a very real sense from this point on this is a matter between Father and Son. With this understanding some of the things that happened over the next 15 hours will make much more sense.

Rather than wait for them to come to Him, Jesus advances to meet the mob. So that there would be no mistake in the darkness, Judas has informed the arresting party that he will identify Jesus by kissing Him, the customary practice of greeting between friends, even down to the present day, in the Middle East.

As Judas approached to kiss Jesus, our Lord asked him, "Judas is it with a kiss that you are betraying the Son of Man?" By using the term messianic term Son of Man, Jesus was giving Judas one final opportunity to recognize Him for who He was.

When Judas failed to respond, Jesus continued, "Friend, do what you are here to do." It is as though Jesus is saying, "OK, Judas, you made your choice. The next time we will meet will be at the Great White Throne Judgment."[11]

> Jesus, in a move to protect His disciples, asks the mob, "Who is it you are looking for?"
>
> They reply, "Jesus, the Nazarene."
>
> Jesus answers, "That's Me." (literally "I am.")

The soldiers then drew back and fell to the ground, reflecting what is probably a supernatural event. But the point is, Jesus is in complete control of the situation.

> Once more Jesus asks, "Who are you looking for?"
>
> "Jesus the Nazarene," they respond.
>
> Jesus confidently and calmly retorts, "I told you, I am He. If therefore you are after Me, let these men go."

At this point the guards, having had the identity of Jesus confirmed, seize Him and take Him into their custody (John 18:12). In a token of resistance on the part of the disciples, Peter takes his sword and slashes at "the servant of the high priest," a man by the name of Malchus. However, he does not issue a fatal blow, and ends up only slicing off the man's ear.

There can be little doubt that Peter intended to kill Malchus in the process of protecting his Friend. On one level I have to admire the courage of Peter, who was a fisherman and not a warrior. But this was not God's will for the moment.

Jesus instructed Peter to put the sword back in its scabbard and then uttered the now-famous saying, "For all who take the sword will by the sword perish." This was no sensible way to proceed, even if it seemed like an appropriate indication of loyalty to Jesus.

If resistance were the right thing, Jesus had no need of swords or human assistance. He makes the statement, in the form of a rhetorical question, that supernatural help is available to him with just a word to his Father.

> "Do you think I cannot call to My Father, and He will put at my disposal more than twelve legions of angels?" (Matthew 26:53).

Twelve legions of angels is an enormous number. A legion of Roman troops, at full strength, was about six thousand men.[12] Twelve legions of angels would have numbered 72,000. One angel would have been enough to rescue Jesus, if that had been the Father's will. By using this massive number Jesus is indicating there is no need for human assistance. God can handle this.

At this point Jesus turned to speak to the mob and accused them of cowardice.

> "Have you come out with swords and clubs to arrest Me as *you would* against a robber? Every day I used to sit in the temple teaching and you did not seize Me" (Matthew 26:55).

He had taught openly in the Temple. Why had they not chosen to arrest Him there?

All of the disciples then deserted Him and fled. They feared for their lives, and for good reason. The soldiers do not chase down the group. They have the one they came after, fulfilling the prophecy. "Strike the Shepherd and the sheep will flee" (Zechariah 13:7). John and Peter eventually circle back and followed the soldiers as they take Jesus to the palace of Caiaphas, which was about a 45 minute walk from the Garden of Gethsemane.

THE RELIGIOUS TRIAL

The religious trial of Jesus occurred in three phases:
1. The examination before Annas (John 18:13-14, 19-23).

2. The examination before Caiaphas (Matthew 26:57, 59-68; Mark 14:53, 55-65; Luke 22:54a, 63-65).

3. The condemnation by the Sanhedrin (Matthew 27:1; Mark 15:1a; Luke 22:66-71).

There were many illegalities of the religious trials of Jesus, the first of which was holding the trial at night.[13]

Upon arrival Jesus was taken to Annas who was the father in law of Caiaphas. Annas apparently had an apartment at the home of the "official" High Priest, Caiaphas. Annas was not High Priest at the time but he was the power behind the scenes. The Romans had used their influence to remove him from office about fifteen years earlier, for what reason we do not know. But the Jews considered the High Priesthood to be a lifetime appointment so he is still referred to in various places after 15AD as the "high priest."

No figure (apart from Jesus) is better known from first century Jewish history than Annas. He was considered successful, but he was also feared and loathed by the common Jew. Annas was a Sadducee. Although the Pharisees and the Sadducees generally despised each other, they hated Jesus more. They were willing to temporarily set aside their differences in order to rid themselves of Jesus, who they considered their common enemy.

The Sadducees, who were more political than religious, hated Jesus because they believed He was upsetting their very fragile political situation with Rome. The Romans allowed some degree of self rule in nations they conquered and the Sadducees, at that point in Jewish history, possessed a measure of political power not shared by others in Israel.

The Pharisees hated Jesus because they believed (rightly so) that He was upsetting the religious status quo. The Pharisees had set themselves up as the standard for righteousness necessary to attain a right standing before God. But Jesus had preached, "Unless your righteousness *exceeds* that of the scribes and Pharisees you shall not enter the kingdom of Heaven." Jesus repeatedly labeled the Pharisees as hypocrites and their system as insufficient for salvation.

Without a doubt, Annas was the political boss in Jerusalem. From a Jewish perspective he was the real power in the world of early first century Israel. So although Annas had no legitimate legal authority, he was ultimately in charge.

Annas had only two questions for Jesus. He asked about Jesus' disciples and His teaching. His desire was to find out how extensive of a following Jesus had. To Annas' frustration, Jesus did not answer the question about His disciples. The Shepherd was not going to endanger His sheep.

As to the question about His teaching Jesus answered,

> "I have always spoken openly to the world; I always taught in the synagogues and in the Temple, where all the Jews come together, and I spoke nothing in secret. Why then do you question Me? Question those who have heard what I spoke to them; behold these know what I said" (John 18:20-21).

Some minor official (probably one of the Jewish temple police) was quick to take exception to Jesus' challenge of Annas, and slapped Jesus on the face. But Jesus did not back down. He basically said, "If I have said something wrong, tell me what it is. If I am wrong, file contempt of court charges against Me. Otherwise, why the assault?"

Here, Jesus gives us a glimpse of what turning the other cheek might look like. He does not accept the injustice silently. Violence in a courtroom was illegal under Jewish law and everyone present knew it. His challenge to this illegality was justified. He had the courage to speak the truth, even in the most distressing of circumstances. He was no coward. Jesus was not the least bit intimidated by this act of violence.

Around 2 AM, Annas realized that he would get nowhere with Jesus and sent Him across the courtyard to Caiaphas. If Jesus is to be brought before the Roman governor, Pontius Pilate, the legal accusation had to be brought by the reigning high priest, Caiaphas, in his capacity as chairman of the Sanhedrin. John noted in his gospel that Jesus remained bound as a criminal even though He had done nothing to warrant physical restraint. These proceedings lasted off and on for the rest of the night. Because the Sanhedrin had been quickly called together, to conduct this "trial" they had no opportunity to prepare witnesses. Once they became somewhat organized the Sanhedrin began calling witnesses against Jesus.

The hypocrisy here is that these men were trying to delude themselves, and everyone else, that they were being fair to Jesus. After all they were, *at least theoretically*, the religious leaders of Israel. They had a reputation to uphold. They could not be perceived as running an illegitimate court. They needed to promote the perception that they were being fair so later they could say, "We gave Him every benefit of the doubt, but He was guilty."

This proceeding lasted for some time, perhaps for hours. Archaeologists have discovered a hole in the floor of what they believe to have been Caiaphas' residence. This hole leads to a room that has no other entrance or exit and it is believed that prisoners were let down by a rope into the room and held there until their testimony was needed. This would prevent their escape. If this is true, *and remember we are going by archaeological evidence and not Biblical evidence,* then it is very possible that Jesus was held in this underground room for portions of the night.

In the meantime a fraudulent trial was taking place. Try as they may they could not find two people to agree on something that Jesus has allegedly done wrong. Witness after witness came forward, in what must have been a very frustrating time for Caiaphas. Here he was trying to quickly obtain a conviction against Jesus and he could not get two people to agree as per the requirements of the Mosaic Law.[14]

Finally two come forward and testified that Jesus claimed to be able to destroy the Temple and rebuild it in three days. An outraged Caiaphas immediately challenged Jesus,

"Are you the Christ, the Son of God?"

"I am," replied Jesus.

Jesus made it clear who He was to His accusers. Some today deny the deity of Christ. Others deny that Jesus ever claimed to be God. Both of those claims are simply not consistent with the Biblical record.[15]

Caiaphas, in a show of insincere indignation tore his clothes and accused Jesus of blasphemy, which was punishable by death under the Mosaic system.[16]

Once Jesus was "convicted" the guards began to brutalize Him. They beat him repeatedly, yet he did not defend Himself. This part of the narrative amazes me every time I think about it. It is one thing to remain silent and allow yourself to be beaten if you can do nothing about it. It is another thing entirely to allow a beating if you are perfectly capable of destroying everyone present with a single thought. Jesus, in His deity, was omnipotent. He could have ended this atrocity in an instant, but he did not. He refused to do so because He was there for a purpose. He refused to save Himself because He came to save us.

Someone, no doubt, pointed out to Caiaphas that under Jewish law the nighttime trial was illegal. Wanting to cover themselves they decided to make their guilty verdict "official" in the daytime and before the full Sanhedrin. It seems very unlikely that they could gather the entire ruling body at that early hour and even more unlikely that Nicodemus and Joseph of Aramathea were invited.

Before the sun had risen and while the streets were still quiet they took Jesus to the Sanhedrin council chamber in the Temple area. The One who had been there indwelling the Holy of Holies as the Shekinah Glory of the Old Testament would now receive His formal rejection by the Jewish leadership very near the same place. The irony here is hard to miss. Here is the beaten and bloodied Son of God, the promised Seed of the Woman standing in what God described to David as a "house for My Name" being convicted of blasphemy.

This was a short meeting as the verdict had already been decided. There was one question:"If you are the Messiah, tell us." Jesus' answer was also brief, "If I tell you, you will not believe."

Jesus knew their hearts were hardened. The way Jesus' response is put in the Greek is very forceful and also very final: "You will never believe."[17] The time for talking was over but still they persisted, "Therefore, you are the Son of God?" Jesus answers, "You are right in saying I am."

We must not miss this important confirmation of Jesus' identity given here. Jesus affirmed that He was the Son of God. Actually, Jesus referred to Himself most frequently during His time on Earth as the "Son of Man." The term "Son of Man" is used of deity in Daniel 7:13. The Jews understood this. The Jewish expectation was that the Messiah would be deity. They were unaware as to how this would come to be, but there was always a Jewish expectation that the Messiah would be divine. It is either pure ignorance of Scripture or pure rejection of Scripture for someone today to say that Jesus never claimed to be God. He did. And the Jews fully understood His claim.

Jesus acknowledged that He was claiming to be God. And He was guilty of blasphemy, that is, unless His claim was true. This is precisely where all of human history turns. All of our understanding of objective reality must be filtered through this claim.Either Jesus is who he said he was or he is not. C. S. Lewis put it this way in his classic, *Mere Christianity*,

> I am trying here to prevent anyone saying the really foolish thing that people often say about Him: I'm ready to accept Jesus as a great moral teacher, but I don't accept his claim to be God. That is the one thing we must not say. A man who was merely a man and said the sort of things Jesus said would not be a great moral teacher. He would either be a lunatic—on the level with the man who says he is a poached egg—or else he would be the Devil of Hell. You must make your choice. Either this man was, and is, the Son of God, or else a madman or something worse. You can shut him up for a fool, you can spit at him and kill him as a demon or you can fall at his feet and call him Lord and God, but let us not come with any patronizing nonsense about his being a great human teacher. He has not left that open to us. He did not intend to.[18]

THE CIVIL TRIALS

Between the hours of 6:00 AM and 9:00 AM there were three civil trials of Jesus of Nazareth. Trials one and three were held before Pontius Pilate, the Roman governor and trial two was a brief one before Herod, the acting king of the Jews.

The Jewish leadership had convicted Jesus of blasphemy. The punishment for blasphemy under Jewish law was death. But the Jewish leadership was in a difficult spot: the Jews were under Roman rule at the time. Even though it happened occasionally (remember Stephen's stoning) the Jews were not allowed to execute anyone. That right/responsibility fell to the Romans. Therefore, to obtain permission to kill Jesus, and to make this perversion of justice "legal," the Jews led Jesus to Pilate.

It was early morning and most of those who were in Jerusalem for the Passover were just waking up. The governor's palace was near the place where the Sanhedrin met so it would have been a short walk.

Evidently the chief priests and elders had to decide how they would present Jesus' case to Pilate to secure the verdict they wanted from him. The title "governor" is a general one. Actually, Pilate was a prefect (procurator) whom Tiberius Caesar had appointed in 26 A.D. Judea and Samaria had become one Roman province in 6 A.D. Normally Pilate resided in Caesarea, but during the Jewish feasts he often came to Jerusalem because it became a potential trouble spot since many thousands of worshippers gathered.

A general understanding of Pilate's political situation would be helpful here so that we might have a better understanding why he would pronounce Jesus not guilty yet still order His execution.

Pilate was operating as prefect of Judea from a position of weakness. He was on "thin ice," as they say, when it came to his relationship to Tiberius. Rome gave the governors of their territories a significant amount of latitude in the administration of the affairs of the region provided nothing happened that would cause the Romans to send additional troops to the area to suppress an uprising. It cost money to move troops and the Romans did not like spending money putting down uprisings.

In the providence of God, Pilate had experienced five incidents with the Jews in his time in Judea that left him in a weakened position. Tiberius had warned Pilate that there should be no more trouble in Judea, or he would hold Pilate responsible.

Incident #1:
Shortly after he arrived in Judea (26 AD), Pilate sent troops in to Jerusalem with images of Caesar attached to poles. He was attempting to show loyalty to Tiberius by doing so but ended up unnecessarily offending the local Jewish population who took the images to be a violation of Jewish law. The Jews protested and after six days Pilate told them he would kill the protestors if they did not go home. They did not leave and Pilate did not kill them. This episode suggests a man who lacked political skills but does not present him as savage tyrant.

Incident #2

While there is no historical evidence of an uprising there were hard feelings over a series of coins that Pilate had minted during the period of 29-31 AD which had pagan cult images imprinted upon them. Again, the Jews considered this a violation of the Mosaic Law.

Incident #3

In order to build a 20-40 mile long aqueduct into Jerusalem Pilate raided the Temple treasury for the money to complete the project. This move was insensitive and rather stupid on Pilate's part. The money he took had been previously designated for social welfare and public works projects but his theft of the funds irritated the Jews to no end. Tens of thousands of Jews surrounded Pilate's residence and threatened to do him serious harm. In response, Pilate sent his men in to the crowd disguised as civilians and on his orders they began to attack the Jews. The soldiers got carried away and there are indicators that they went beyond what Pilate ordered. Large numbers of Jews were killed directly by the soldiers and many others were trampled to death when the crowd tried to flee. Again, in this incident, things got out of control against Pilate's wishes.

Incident #4:

During the time of Jesus' public ministry Pilate had some Galileans killed and mingled their blood with the blood of their sacrifices in the Temple (Luke 13:1). While there were not many people involved in this brutality, it created a great deal of ill will. Some point to this as the beginning of enmity between Pilate and Herod Antipas, the Tetrarch of Galilee.

Incident #5

Not that long before Jesus' crucifixion Pilate dedicated shields coated with gold at the palace of Herod in Jerusalem. There were no images on the shields but the Jews were offended nevertheless, because there were names on the shields, which they still considered idolatrous. By this time the Jews had become hypersensitive and Pilate was quickly losing support in Rome over what Emperor Tiberius perceived as weak leadership.[19]

Pilate's ability to stand up to the Jews had been severely damaged. He had trouble with Rome on the one hand and with the Jews on the other. The Jews were very aware of his weakened position. That is why they were able to bully Pilate into executing a man that he knew was innocent.

Pilate was surely aware of Jesus' arrest. After all, he had provided some of the soldiers for the arrest at Gethsemane. But he probably thought that the Jews would take care of this matter "in house." There would be no need for any further involvement on his part. I suspect that Pilate was quite irritated at being drawn into this.

The Jewish mob that brought Jesus to Pilate stayed outside the governor's residence because they wanted to avoid ceremonial defilement. In their duplicity they didn't want to be defiled by entering a Gentile dwelling on the Passover. Ironically, these Jews were taking extreme precautions to avoid ritual defilement while at the same time preparing to murder the promised Messiah that would "take away the sins of the world." It seems that this pattern has been followed many times in the course of human history. Far too often evil has been committed in the name of God.

Jesus celebrated the Passover meal with His disciples the evening before His arrest. Why then does John indicate that the Jews did not want to be defiled so as to be unable to "eat the Passover?" Many solutions have been proposed but in my view, the one with the least difficulties is proposed by D.A. Carson,

> The "Passover" was the name that the Jews used to describe both the Passover proper and the entire festival that followed it including the feast of Unleavened Bread. Evidently it was their continuing participation in this eight-day festival that these Jewish leaders did not want to sacrifice by entering a Gentile residence.[20]

The Jews refused to enter Pilate's residence so he came out to them at around 6:00 AM and asked, "What charge do you bring against this man?"

"If he were not a criminal we would not have brought him to you," they answer.

"If there is no formal charge, then take him and judge him yourselves," Pilate responds.

"We have no right to execute anyone," the Jews replied.

The Jews insist that Jesus is guilty of "many things." He stirs up trouble, He is subverting the nation, He opposes payment of taxes to Caesar and claims to be the Messiah, a king. Pilate then returned inside and challenged Jesus.

"Are you the king of the Jews?" he demanded.

"Is that your idea or did someone tell that to you?" Jesus replied.

"Am I a Jew? What have you done?"

"My kingdom is not of this world. If it were my servants would fight to prevent my arrest. But now my kingdom is not of this world."

"You are a king then?" Pilate asked.

"Yes, it is for that reason I was born, to testify to the truth. Everyone on the side of truth listens to Me."

"What is truth?" Pilate responded in exasperation.

When Pilate questioned Jesus again. Jesus did not answer.

Pilate returned to the crowd and declared, "I find no basis for a charge against Him."

At 6:30 AM, Pilate, looking for a way out of this, heard that Jesus was from Galilee, and sent Jesus to Herod, who was in Jerusalem at the time. The scene at Herod's residence was maddening with Herod shooting questions at Jesus asking Him to perform miracles and the Jews constantly accusing Him. Through this ordeal, Jesus remained silent. Finally, receiving no response from Jesus, Herod sent Him back to Pilate.

Pilate attempted to allow everyone to save face by offering to release either Jesus or Barabbas, a man convicted of murder and insurrection. The Jews chose Barabbas. Pilate, stunned by the irrationality of the mob, asks them to change their mind. They say no, and demand, "Crucify Him! Crucify Him!"

"Why?" asked Pilate.

They answer again, even more loudly, "Crucify Him!"

Pilate, wanting to get out of this if he can, had Jesus scourged. Some scholars believe that this is the first of two scourgings that Jesus endured that morning.[21] This one, while brutal, was less severe than the one He will receive right before He is taken to be crucified. After the initial scourging Jesus is then brought before the crowd. Pilate cries out "Behold the Man!" Again, hoping the crowd would be satisfied with the punishment. But they were not.

They continued to yell, "Crucify Him!"

Pilate answered, "You crucify Him for I find no basis for a charge against Him."

In the frenzy the Jews responded, "We have a law and under the law He must die because He claimed to be the Son of God!"

It is at this point that fear takes hold of Pilate like it had not before. He had concerns before, to be sure, but now, he knows he is in between the proverbial rock and hard place. He returns to the palace and questions Jesus, "Where are you from?" He is beginning to see that the Man before Him is not merely a simple carpenter from Galilee. There is something more here.

Jesus does not answer. Pilate becomes more disturbed.

He challenges Jesus, "Do you refuse to speak to me? Don't you realize that I have the power to either free you or crucify you?"

Jesus boldly replies, "You would have no power over Me if it were not given to you from above. Therefore the one who handed Me over to you (the Jewish leadership) is guilty of a greater sin."[22]

Pilate tried again to set Jesus free but the mob would have none of it. They yelled, "If you release Him you are no friend of Caesar. Anyone who claims to be a king opposes Caesar."

Pilate then sits on the judge's seat and has Jesus brought out before the crowd. He presents Jesus to the mob and says, "Here is your king!"

But they shouted, "Take Him away, crucify Him!"

"Shall I crucify your king?" Pilate asked.

"We have no king but Caesar!" they responded.

Pilate then surrendered to the pressure. He washed his hands in front of the crowd and declared, "I am innocent of this man's blood. It is your responsibility."

"Let His blood be upon us and our children," they countered.

Pilate then handed Jesus over for the more severe flogging, one that was commonly administered right before crucifixion. Jesus was stripped naked and tied to a pole and then beaten without mercy with a whip made of leather strips with pieces of metal and bone intertwined in the strips. Ancient eyewitness accounts of this kind of scourging, *verberatio*, administered by the Romans relate that the individual's flesh was torn from his body, often to the point of the intestines becoming visible. There is no reason to believe that Jesus suffered any less.

Following the beating Jesus was mocked and ridiculed by the Roman soldiers. They dressed Him in a purple robe and pounded a crown of thorns into His scalp. "Hail, King of the Jews," they taunted as they punched Him repeatedly in the face.

Throughout all of this Jesus exercised the greatest restraint that has ever been exercised. He could have stopped all of this with one thought, with one word. All of those who were torturing Him would have dropped dead immediately. It would have all been over. But had he done so, it would also have been all over for you and for me as well. There would be no hope of salvation and we would all be on our way to Hell.

He refused to save Himself because His mission was to save you and me. And He was determined to complete His mission regardless of the pain that He had to endure along the way. He was going to die on the Cross and nothing was going to stop Him.

Think about that the next time you feel unloved, unappreciated or despised. Jesus, the very Creator of the universe, endured the scourgings, the beatings, the ridicule and the scorn because He loves you. He loves you with a loyal love that will not let you go.

And now, the suffering intensifies.

THE CRUCIFIXION OF JESUS CHRIST

C. Truman Davis a medical doctor provides a physical description of Roman Crucifixion:

> The cross is placed on the ground and the exhausted man is quickly thrown backwards with his shoulders against the wood. The legionnaire feels for the depression at the front of the wrist. He drives a heavy, square wrought-iron nail through the wrist and deep into the wood. Quickly he moves to the other side and repeats the action, being careful not to pull the arms too tightly, but to allow some flex and movement. The cross is then lifted into place.

> The left foot is pressed backward against the right foot, and with both feet extended, toes down, a nail is driven through the arch of each, leaving the knees flexed. The victim is now crucified. As he slowly sags down with more weight on the nails in the wrists, excruciating, fiery pain shoots along the fingers and up the arms to explode in the brain—the nails in the wrists are putting pressure on the median nerves. As he pushes himself upward to avoid this stretching torment, he places the full weight on the nail through his feet. Again he feels the searing agony of the nail tearing through the nerves between the bones of his feet.

> As the arms fatigue, cramps sweep through the muscles, knotting them in deep, relentless, throbbing pain. With these cramps comes the inability to push himself upward to breathe. Air can be drawn into the lungs, but not exhaled. He fights to raise himself in order to get even one small breath. Finally carbon dioxide builds up in the lungs and in the blood stream, and the cramps partially subside. Spasmodically he is able to push himself upward to exhale and bring in life-giving oxygen.

Hours of this limitless pain, cycles of twisting, joint-rending cramps, intermittent partial asphyxiation, searing pain as tissue is torn from his lacerated back as he moves up and down against the rough timber. Then another agony begins: a deep, crushing pain deep in the chest as the pericardium slowly fills with serum and begins to compress the heart.

It is now almost over—the loss of tissue fluids has reached a critical level—the compressed heart is struggling to pump heavy, thick, sluggish blood into the tissues—the tortured lungs are making a frantic effort to gasp in small gulps of air.

He can feel the chill of death creeping through his tissues… Finally he can allow his body to die. All this the Bible records with the simple words, 'And they crucified Him.' (Mark 15:24).[23]

The brutal scourgings that our Lord endured put Him in a position of extreme physical weakness. As the procession made its way through the streets on the way to Golgotha (also called the "Hill of the Skull"), located outside the city wall of Jerusalem where the execution was readily visible to all who entered and exited the city, many followed along. It was customary for the Romans to require the prisoner condemned to execution to carry his own cross. This was a further form of humiliation. Historical research shows that most commonly, the prisoner carried only the upper cross bar, rather than the whole cross. The upright portion of the cross awaited the condemned at the sight of execution.

In His weakened condition the weight of the cross was too much for Jesus to bear and He fell under its weight. The Roman soldiers compelled a bystander, Simon of Cyrene, to carry it for Jesus the remainder of the distance to the Hill of the Skull. Two others, who were criminals, were part of the procession.

Once they arrived at the place of execution Jesus was offered a drink of wine mixed with myrrh. Matthew records that He tasted it but then refused to drink it. This is traditionally understood to be a drink that would dull the senses, as per the Jewish custom (Proverbs 31:6-7), but a small sip of wine would hardly kill the pain of one who had been scourged and myrrh has only mild analgesic properties. In addition, this was a *Jewish* custom and the Romans were in charge at the moment. It is more likely that this was a further example of the contempt by the Romans and Jesus refuses to participate. They are pretending to be kind, when in fact they are simply mocking Him.

At approximately 9:00 AM, Jesus was crucified between the two criminals. As the Lord of the universe hangs between heaven and earth, the soldiers gamble for His outer garment. The Romans ordinarily crucified their prisoners naked. Christian tradition has it that because Jesus' mother was present, the Romans made an exception and allowed Him to retain a loincloth. I seriously doubt this. It doesn't sound consistent with their attitude toward Jesus. They had mocked Him and beaten Him without mercy. It is doubtful that He was allowed this small act of dignity. It is possible but not probable.

Pilate ordered an inscription to be placed at the top of Jesus' cross that read in Hebrew, Latin and in Greek, "Jesus the Nazarene, King of the Jews." The Jews protested this to Pilate, but Pilate refused to change it. He had had enough of the Jewish leadership.

THE SEVEN DECLARATIONS OF JESUS FROM THE CROSS

The Gospels record seven things Jesus said on the Cross. They are all significant.

The first declaration:
As the soldiers gambled for his garment, Jesus uttered the first saying, "Father, forgive them for they know not what they do" (Luke 23:34).

Under Roman custom, four soldiers under the leadership of a centurion were assigned to each of the persons being executed. While the immediate contrast is between Jesus' concern for his executioners and their disregard of him (as they cast lots for portions of his clothing), the scope of the prayer reaches to all who had a hand in securing Jesus' present position upon the cross. What an incredible attitude! No threats, no defiant words. Just forgiveness.

The soldiers continued to mock Jesus, however, challenging, "If you are the King of the Jews, save yourself."

The second declaration:

"Truly I say to you, today you shall be with Me in Paradise" (Luke 23:43).

Matthew records that both of the criminals crucified with Jesus insulted Him. But while the first of the criminals continued the verbal barrage on Our Lord, the other had a change of heart. As recorded in Luke 23:39-43 the man recognized his need, he exercised faith and he was justified before God, his sins were forgiven and he received eternal life.

Please notice this unnamed criminal was not in a position to undergo baptism, to perform good works, to join a church, or to give money. All he could do was place his faith in Jesus as the covenanted Messiah to Israel, the only way to the Father.

The third declaration:

"Woman behold thy Son ... behold thy mother"(John 19:26-27).

Christ's care for His mother is seen in this third saying from the Cross. Even though Jesus' brothers (the physical children of Mary and Joseph) would normally have been expected to take care of their mother, they were at this time, unbelievers. Jesus turned the care of His mother over to John, His trusted disciple and perhaps one of his two best friends, humanly speaking. History records that the Apostle John did indeed care for Mary until her death.

Calling His mother "Woman" (*gune*) was not a sign of disrespect. It was the normal form of address from an older son to a mother at that time and in that culture.

John mentions that there were four women on hand at the Crucifixion of Jesus. They stand in strict contrast with the soldiers that are present. While the soldiers carry out their barbaric task and gamble without apology for our Lord's outer garment, (as D. A. Carson put it) the women "wait in faithful devotion to the One whose death they cannot understand at this point as anything but a tragedy."

Mary, Jesus' mother, knew the theology behind what is happening. She had known from the beginning. But I doubt, at this point, that she was thinking of the doctrines of unlimited atonement, propiti-ation or reconciliation. Rather, she watched in horror as she saw her

Son brutalized by godless men. I'm sure there were more than a few flashbacks to a time that seemed like yesterday, when He was but an infant in her arms. She had been told when He was a newborn that her soul would be pierced. And it was.

Supporting Mary during this unspeakable ordeal were Mary's sister, Salome, (Jesus' aunt and very probably, according to many NT scholars, the mother of James and John, making Jesus, James and John first cousins), as well as Mary, wife of Clopas and Mary Magdalene.

We have just seen that the first three hours of His crucifixion, Jesus Christ uttered these statements.

- Father forgive them for they know not what they do.
- Today you will be with Me in Paradise
- Woman behold Thy Son, Behold thy Mother.

In these statements Our Lord:

- Expressed His grace.
- Demonstrated that no one is too evil to go to Heaven, provided they exercise faith in the right object, Jesus.
- Saw to the continuing care of His mother.

At 12:00 noon to 3:00 PM "darkness fell over the whole land" (Luke 23:44).

Up until this time the Scriptures record nothing of any screams of pain on Jesus' part. Yes, there might have been cries of pain when the nails pierced His hands and feet. It hurt terribly. And the pain from the scourging would have been unbearable. But nothing is recorded of Jesus crying out in pain. However, shortly after noon a scream pierced the darkness and the tense of the Greek verb (the imperfect) indicates that Jesus probably uttered this cry over and over.

The fourth declaration:

> *Eloi, Eloi, lama sabachthani?* which is translated: "My God, My God, why have you forsaken Me?" (Mark 15:34).

Jesus is quoting Psalm 22 in this cry of agony.

Here's where the suffering intensifies. As hard as it might be to believe, everything up to now has been in the category of preliminaries. Now, Jesus incurs the wrath of God for the sins of the world. Now, He pays the price demanded by a holy God for those deeds we would rather call "errors in judgment" or "poor decisions." Now, He is punished for what we do so flippantly so often and with such frequency that it becomes routine. *Now, Jesus screams.*

The question was of course, rhetorical. He knew why He was being forsaken. He had agreed to this in eternity past.

> He who knew no sin was being made sin for us that we through Him might be made the righteousness of God in Him (2 Corinthians 5:21).

Here Jesus enters spiritual death, separation from God, in some indescribable way as the sinner's substitute. His physical death followed shortly after His spiritual death.

The exact nature of the Father's forsaking of the Son has long troubled thoughtful students of the Word of God. How can deity forsake deity? Or, how can deity abandon deity? God did not choose to reveal to us the mystery of the specifics of this separation. All we can say with certainty is that the Father poured out His wrath upon the Son for the sins we committed. Because of the work of Christ on the Cross, the Father will never forsake the believer, even when we sin. Jesus paid the penalty so we would never be forsaken.[24]

Some of those standing there who heard Jesus cry misunderstood the Aramaic *Eloi,* for the name for Elijah and concluded that He was calling upon the prophet for help. But no, Elijah could not help Jesus. This was an issue between two members of the Holy Trinity. It was a matter between Father and Son that had been decided upon long ago in eternity past. It had been decreed that the Father would judge His Son for my sins and for yours. And Jesus screamed in agony.

The fifth declaration:

After a period of three hours, Jesus said, "I thirst" John 19:28 (an apparent reference to Psalm 69:21).

Jesus had been on the Cross for six hours by this time. He had endured brutal beatings beforehand. His body was greatly dehydrated. Loss of fluid, from sweat and some blood loss would explain this extreme thirst. From a jar of wine vinegar that was nearby someone lifted a sponge full on a branch of hyssop to His lips and wet His mouth. This was one of the few acts of mercy shown the Lord of the universe as He suffered this horrible death. It is probable that Jesus received this drink to moisten his mouth so the next saying would not be misunderstood.

The sixth declaration:
Once Jesus' mouth was moistened, He uttered what is perhaps the most theologically significant of all of the sayings, "It is finished." (Greek, *Tetelestai*)

The mission had been accomplished. Jesus had completed the work that He had been sent to do. The work of salvation was finished. Completed. There was and is nothing that can be added to it. To attempt to, as so many do, is blasphemy of the highest degree.

The work of Christ on the Cross renders all men savable

The payment Jesus made to satisfy the Father was for all sins committed by all men. No sin was left out. Not Moses' anger or David's adultery or Paul's persecution of Christians. All sins. All of the sins I have ever committed or ever will and all the sins you have or ever will commit.

The work of Christ on the Cross renders all men savable. Christ paid the penalty for all. But that payment has not been applied to all. Application of the payment awaits faith on the part of the individual. Until then, to use Paul's terminology in Ephesians 2:1, you remain "dead in your trespasses and sins."

The seventh declaration:
Luke 23:46 reports that His final words on the Cross were a quotation of Psalm 31:5a, "Father into your hands I deposit My Spirit."

All having been accomplished, Jesus exhaled and allowed His Spirit to rejoin the Father. Christ died because by an act of His will; He dismissed His Spirit from His body. Christ was sovereign over His death. I'm sure that Satan and the enemies of Jesus thought they had just won a great victory. But that was hardly the case. The promised Seed of the Woman had crushed the Seed of the Serpent. James Stewart, a minister of the Church of Scotland, put it well,

> The very triumphs of His foes, He used for their defeat. He compelled their dark achievements to sub-serve His end, not theirs. They nailed Him to the tree, not knowing that by that very act they were bringing the world to His feet. They gave Him a cross, not guessing that He would make it a throne. They flung Him outside the gates to die, not knowing that in that very moment they were lifting up all the gates of the universe, to let the King of Glory come in.
>
> They thought to root out His doctrines, not understanding that they were implanting imperishably in the hearts of men the very name they intended to destroy. They thought they had defeated God with His back to the wall, pinned and helpless and defeated: they did not know that it was God Himself who had tracked them down. He did not conquer in spite of the dark mystery of evil. He conquered through it.[25]

The Cross was not a defeat. It was God's consummate victory. Three days later Jesus was resurrected from the dead demonstrating to all the Father's satisfaction with the work of Jesus.

The cost of our redemption from sin was enormous. Salvation is free to us, but it cost God everything.

Chapter 4 Summary

■ The Crucifixion and Resurrection of Jesus was the central and defining event in all of human history.

■ While we may not have a full appreciation of the Crucifixion and Resurrection of Jesus until we see Him in Eternity, it is certainly beneficial to spend time on this side of Heaven considering this event that is central to the reality of forgiveness.

■ At the Cross the promised Seed of the Woman crushed the Seed of the Serpent.

Something to Consider

The first Bible verse many children learn begins, "For God so loved the world…" We read the words but the full meaning doesn't come close to becoming a reality until we have some understanding of the magnitude of the sacrifice God made for us. God did not choose some unknown angel, who lived in some remote part of the universe, who had no friends or family, who would not be missed, to die as a substitute for sinful man. He chose His eternal Son with whom He had enjoyed eternal fellowship. He gave that which was most dear to Him to fulfill a need we could never meet on our own. Think about that the next time you feel unloved or unappreciated. God the Father gave up everything for you. God the Son, Jesus, died in your place. That's how much you are loved. Charles Wesley put it so well when he wrote,

Amazing love! How can it be
That Thou my God should die for me?

What Must I Do?

❖ ❖ ❖

"Jesus Christ came not to condemn you but to save you, knowing your name, knowing all about you, knowing your weight right now, knowing your age, knowing what you do, knowing where you live, knowing what you ate for supper and what you will eat for breakfast, where you will sleep tonight, how much your clothing cost, who your parents were. He knows you individually as though there were not another person in the entire world. He died for you as certainly as if you had been the only lost one. He knows the worst about you and is the One who loves you the most."   *A. W. Tozer*

❖ ❖ ❖

Over two millennia ago, a jailer in the ancient Greek town of Philippi asked the apostle Paul a question that has reverberated throughout the centuries:

"What must I do to be saved?"

The answer was short and to the point. "Believe on the Lord Jesus." The answer Paul gave is just as valid today as it was that night 2000 years ago.

This unnamed man understood he had a need. He was in a state of desperation and was acutely aware that without help he would remain in deep trouble. He knew that should he die that night, there was no chance he would end up in Heaven. He simply wasn't good enough.

I doubt that Paul's answer was what the jailer was anticipating. Perhaps he expected Paul to tell him he needed to clean up his life immediately and begin living in a way that would please God. Maybe he needed to apologize for mistreating the prisoners in his care and promise never to do that again. That is what a lot of people today would have prescribed. But that is not what Paul told him.

In the Greek text from which we get our English translations, the word translated as "believe" can also be rendered "trust." This jailer needed to simply trust Jesus Christ for the forgiveness of his sins, and he would receive eternal life. He would be "saved." The solution to his problem was simple but profound. *Faith alone in Christ alone.*

We have a need that we cannot meet in and of ourselves

The Scriptures tell us that we were all born physically alive but spiritually dead. And to confirm that status, all of us have done things that we know are not consistent with the character of a holy God. All have sinned and fall short of the glory of God.

We have a need that we cannot meet in and of ourselves. God is perfectly holy; we are not. And because God is holy, He can only have a positive relationship with those who share His righteousness. No amount of behavior rehabilitation can make us as righteous as God. Try as we may, we can never be good enough to get to Heaven.

Since God is just, as well as holy, someone had to pay the penalty for the sins of that jailer as well as everyone who has ever lived. Jesus Christ was our substitute. He paid the penalty that was due each of us.

Now, God offers forgiveness from the penalty of sin and the free gift of eternal life to those who will simply place their faith in Jesus Christ.

No amount of good works will ever get you to Heaven. The only way you'll get there is through Jesus Christ. *Faith alone in Christ alone.* This decision is too important to put off. Simply open your heart and tell God that you know you have sinned and fallen short of His holy standard and that you are trusting Jesus Christ apart from any work on your part to save you. Come to God with empty hands of faith.

God loves you. He wants very much for you to spend eternity with Him. Please don't delay. Do it today. ***Do it now.***

"For God so loved the world that He gave His only begotten Son, that whoever believes in Him shall not perish, but have eternal life" (John 3:16).

"For this is the will of My Father, that everyone who beholds the Son and believes in Him will have eternal life, and I Myself will raise him up on the last day" (John 6:40).

"Jesus said to her, 'I am the resurrection and the life; he who believes in Me will live even if he dies, and everyone who lives and believes in Me will never die'" (John 11: 25-26).

"Believe on the Lord Jesus, and you will be saved..." (Acts 16:31).

"For by grace you have been saved through faith; and that not of yourselves, it is the gift of God; not as a result of works, so that no one may boast" (Ephesians 2:8-9).

The Effect of Sin ...
Before and After Salvation

❖ ❖ ❖

A guilty conscience needs no accuser
Anonymous

❖ ❖ ❖

W**hile psychologists speak** of "guilt feelings" the Scriptures paint a clear picture that all men are *actually* guilty of violating God's moral law. It is not simply feelings of guilt that we must face but the reality of *real guilt*. This real guilt the Bible calls "sin."

THE EFFECT OF SIN BEFORE SALVATION

Sin has been defined in various ways but this one best combines accuracy with ease of remembrance: sin is "any thought, word or deed that violates God's holy standard."

Since God is perfectly holy it would be a violation of His very nature for Him to fellowship with that which violates His holiness. His perfect righteousness and justice demand that He condemn sin, that is, if He is to act rationally, if He is to act consistently with who He is. And God is always rational. He always acts consistently with His own character. And so, we were all born with a problem too great for any of us to solve on our own.

We are sinful. God is perfectly holy. We need a remedy for our sin that we cannot provide for ourselves. Without solving the "sin problem" we will live out our lives and go to our physical death in a state of sin and condemnation. God's holiness demands that sin be punished. That punishment or judgment was accomplished on the Cross, as was discussed in Chapter 4. God the Father poured out His wrath against sin when He judged His Son, Jesus Christ, on the Cross.

As Jesus cried out "My God, My God, why have you forsaken Me?" He knew perfectly well why the Father was forsaking Him. It was part of God's eternal plan with reference to the "sin problem."

> Surely our grief He himself bore,
> And our sorrows He carried. (Isa 53:4)

Jesus did not sin. He was "*made* sin." Our sins were imputed to Him and judged. So, rather than God the Father judging each of us individually for our rebellion, He judged His Son in our place.

Jesus died as a substitute for each of us. He paid the price for our disobedience. And at the moment we place our faith in Him, God the Father takes the finished work of Christ on the Cross and applies it to our account and we are forgiven.

Forgiveness in this sense means that we have been spared the penalty that was due us—eternal death: eternal separation from God and His blessing. The one who places his faith in Jesus will never have to pay that penalty. Jesus paid it for us and we, who have placed our faith in Him, have received the benefit of that payment.

This is the forgiveness Peter was referencing in Acts 10:43 when he said, "Of Him, [speaking of Jesus] all the prophets bear witness that through His name everyone who believes in Him receives the forgiveness of sins."

Judgment of sin occurred at the Cross. Forgiveness from the eternal penalty of sin awaits the moment of faith on the part of the individual. This is crucial and far too often misunderstood. The atoning work of Jesus Christ was *sufficient* for every person who has ever taken a breath on this earth. But the work of Christ is *efficient* only for those who believe.

Again, "everyone *who believes in Him* receives the forgiveness of sins." Norman Geisler put it this way,

> The actual cancelling of the debt is conditional upon belief, i.e. upon actual acceptance of it. Hence, there is no contradiction when there is no forgiveness of those who choose to attempt

to pay their own debt. Likewise those who are forgiven do not have to pay their own debt, since Christ's payment has been applied to them.[26]

None of us has earned the right of forgiveness

It should go without saying that no fallen, sinful, depraved, rebellious human being deserves to be forgiven. None of us earned the right of forgiveness. On the contrary, all of us are the recipients of incredible compassion, mercy and grace on the part of God. Our freedom, our forgiveness was purchased by the substitutionary death of the Son of God through no merit of our own.

I need to make something very clear here: if you have never placed your faith in the Person and Work of Jesus then, according to the Scriptures you are at this present time, "dead in your trespasses and sins."

Challenging the Pharisees, Jesus said,

> "I go away, and you will seek Me, and will die in your sin; where I am going, you cannot come." So the Jews were saying, "Surely He will not kill Himself, will He, since He says, 'Where I am going, you cannot come'?" And He was saying to them, "You are from below, I am from above; you are of this world, I am not of this world. Therefore I said to you that you will die in your sins; for unless you believe that I am *He*, you will die in your sins" (John 8:21-24).

Paul, referencing the time before the Ephesians had trusted Christ wrote, "And you were dead in your trespasses and sins" (Eph 2:1).

The one who has not trusted Jesus is physically alive, but spiritually dead and remains under the condemnation and wrath of God. Forgiveness from the eternal penalty of sin awaits the moment of faith on the individual's part. God did all the work, you simply need to receive the benefits of that work by humbling yourself and being honest with God, recognizing your need and admitting that only He can meet it.

When God forgives us from the eternal penalty of sin it means that He has cancelled the debt, that we are no longer under condemnation and that He will never act again in condemnation or wrath with respect to the individual who has "received the forgiveness of sins."

THE EFFECT SIN HAS ON THE BELIEVER

Paul opens the 8th chapter of his letter to the Romans, "There is therefore now no condemnation to those who are in Christ Jesus."

The phrase "in Christ Jesus" is a favorite Pauline phrase for a person who has placed their faith in Jesus Christ.

Please indulge me as I repeat this one more time, when you place your faith in Christ you receive the forgiveness of sins, which means that you have been spared the eternal penalty of sin. You will never have to pay it. Jesus paid the penalty on the Cross and you have received the benefit of that payment by grace through faith. You have a positional relationship with God that cannot be broken by anything, including any sin committed after salvation.

But are there any consequences for us individually after salvation, after we have received forgiveness from the eternal penalty of sin? This is a fair question.

Salvation once gained cannot be lost

Some in the history of Christian thought have been troubled by the concept that complete forgiveness from the eternal penalty of sin might give people the idea that they can sin after salvation with no consequence at all. They have reacted to that idea and concluded that if one sins after salvation they will again fall under condemnation.

You've heard it, I'm sure. "If you teach that once you are saved you will never again fall under the wrath of God then you are giving people a license to sin." So they manufacture the idea that as a consequence of post salvation sinning one might lose their salvation. Those who teach that admit it is difficult to quantify the amount of sinning necessary to fall again under the wrath of God, but they are convinced nevertheless that it is true.

I have found that the people who hold to this are generally well meaning and their real motivation is to protect the integrity of God and His plan from abuses, but unfortunately they are misinformed.

A careful study of the Word of God would reveal that salvation once gained cannot be lost. A person who has been justified can never lose that justification. Once forgiven the eternal penalty of sin you cannot be "unforgiven." (See appendix)

Yes, as a believer you are secure in your relationship to God. But are there consequences to post salvation sinning? Certainly. Sin causes the believer to lose his closeness with God, referred to in the Scriptures as our fellowship relationship with Him and sin carries with it potential discipline.

The Greek term *koinonia*, most often translated "fellowship" in our English Bibles can also mean, "communion, association, or close relationship."[27] It was a favorite term used by Greek writers outside the Bible to describe the marriage relationship as the most intimate of all relationships.

There are two aspects to a marriage relationship: the legal and the experiential. When a couple stands before a minister or a judge and says, "I do" the one presiding over the ceremony pronounces the couple "husband and wife." He then signs the marriage license and sends it off to the appropriate governmental department for recording. That couple has entered into a legal relationship recognized by God and the government. But all would agree that there is much more to a marriage than simply the legal relationship. There is also a *koinonia* or fellowship relationship.

A couple can be legally married but not in fellowship with each other. All married couples have experienced this. When two people, both possessing sinful natures, live together for any length of time there will inevitably be occasions when the closeness of the relationship is not consistent. People disappoint each other and it interrupts the intimacy of the relationship. But most often when one party or the other simply apologizes for whatever offense led to the break in fellowship all is forgiven and the closeness is restored.

Throughout the period where fellowship had been broken the couple remains in the legal relationship. They remained married. That was not lost. It was the intimacy within the marriage that was lost. It was the joy of the relationship that was lost. And it is the joy of the relationship that returns with a straightforward "I'm sorry." At least, that is the way it ought to work.

We have a similar relationship with God. When we place our faith in Jesus Christ we enter into a permanent, unbreakable relationship with the Almighty. This is analogous to the legal relationship of a marriage. The illustration is not perfect, of course. No illustration is. Marriages can end in divorce, thus dissolving the legal aspect of the relationship. But God will never divorce you, nor can you divorce Him. You will always be in a legal relationship with Him no matter how much you disappoint Him.

The death Jesus died on the Cross paid the eternal penalty of sin and that payment is irrevocable. Once the work of Christ on the Cross is applied to the individual, that person finds themself in a legal relationship that will last forever. God's righteousness and justice have been satisfied.

But while we cannot lose our legal relationship with God, we can and do, on occasion, lose our fellowship relationship with Him. God is holy, meaning that He is completely without sin (1 John 1:5). God's holiness is characterized by His righteousness and absolute moral purity. And in this sense He is totally and absolutely set apart from His fallen creation.

And as stated earlier in this chapter, that which is holy cannot fellowship with that which is not. The Apostle John put it this way in his first epistle, "If we say we have fellowship with Him and yet walk in the darkness, we lie and do not practice the truth" (1 John 1:6).

At this point it would be helpful to remember that the Gospel of John is the only book in the Bible that has as its expressed purpose in the text the evangelization of the unbeliever. (John 20:31) John's Gospel is organized around seven signs that Jesus performed to demonstrate that He was indeed the covenanted Messiah to Israel and the Savior of the world.

The Gospel of John was written primarily to unbelievers as a presentation of the good news of salvation through Jesus. This does not mean that believers cannot benefit from the study of the Gospel of John. We can and certainly do. But it was primarily written to unbelievers as a gospel tract. And in the Gospel of John there is but one condition given for the receiving of forgiveness from the eternal penalty of sin and receiving of eternal life and that is faith alone in Christ alone.

On the other hand, John's epistles were written to people who were already believers in Jesus Christ. The epistles were penned, not to show people how to receive eternal life, but to show us how to live in such a way as to enjoy fellowship with the God with whom we have a positional relationship. In the Gospel of John Jesus said. "I came that they may have life and have it abundantly" (John 10:10b). In his first epistle John expresses what that abundant life looks like and how we can enjoy our salvation.

So we must be careful to keep this straight. 1 John is written to people who were already believers, not to explain to them how to be saved. If we remember this it will save us from making unnecessary mistakes in the application of this great epistle.

When we sin as believers we do not come under condemnation once again. We do not lose our legal relationship with God. But we do lose something. We lose that closeness with God that we were designed to have as his child. We lose our fellowship with Him.

Chapter 6 Summary

■ Once we place our faith in Christ we enter into a positional relationship with God that cannot be broken.

■ The eternal consequence of our sin has been forever forgiven.

■ There are continuing consequences to sins committed after salvation.

■ We do not lose our eternal life when we sin after salvation but we lose the closeness with God we were designed to enjoy.

Something to Consider

Far too many Christians live in constant fear that someday they will do something, say something or think something that will cause God to stop loving them and cancel their salvation. But please remember, as a believer you are God's beloved child and nothing can separate you from His love. It is true that there are consequences to post salvation sins, but the consequences do not include loss of your status as a child of God. You will lose fellowship, but not position. And as there is a divine plan for forgiveness from the eternal penalty of sin, there is a plan for forgiveness from the consequences of post salvation sins. That remedy will be the subject of the next chapter.

Confession

❖ ❖ ❖

The truth is that, properly understood, confession is a key strength of the Christian faith and a vital part of countering hypocrisy. For a start, open voluntary confession is a part and parcel of a strong and comprehensive view of truth, and therefore of realism and responsibilities.

Os Guiness

❖ ❖ ❖

When my brother Tom was young he had an experience that I suspect is pretty universal. He had been playing outside in the rain like little boys do and not just in the rain, but in every mud puddle he could find, and then decided to make his way home. When he arrived, there was my mother, standing at the front door like the Queen's guard at Buckingham Palace.

"Just where do you think you're going?" Mom demanded.

"Inside," Tom answered.

"Not like that you're not. You'll track mud all over my clean house. You take those shoes off and wash up first!"

"Outside?"

"Yes, outside. You take one step into this house like that and you will wish you hadn't!"

I suspect Mom's reaction was typical of mothers all over the world. You don't bring mud into a clean house.

In an infinitely more sophisticated way our Lord, on the night before His Crucifixion, used a similar story to teach a lesson on temporal, post salvation cleansing. Jesus introduces the topic in John.

Now before the Feast of the Passover, Jesus knowing that His hour had come that He would depart
out of this world to the Father, having loved His
own who were in the world, He loved them to the
end. During supper, the devil having already put
into the heart of Judas Iscariot, the son of Simon,
to betray Him, Jesus, knowing that the Father had
given all things into His hands, and that He had
come forth from God and was going back to God,
got up from supper, and laid aside His garments;
and taking a towel, He girded Himself.

Then He poured water into the basin, and began
to wash the disciples' feet and to wipe them with
the towel with which He was girded. So He came
to Simon Peter. He said to Him, "Lord, do You wash
my feet?" Jesus answered and said to him, "What
I do you do not realize now, but you will understand hereafter." Peter said to Him, "Never shall
You wash my feet!" Jesus answered him, "If I do
not wash you, you have no part with Me." Simon
Peter said to Him, "Lord, then wash not only my
feet, but also my hands and my head." Jesus said
to him, "He who has bathed needs only to wash
his feet, but is completely clean; and you are clean,
but not all of you." For He knew the one who was
betraying Him; for this reason He said, "Not all of
you are clean" (John 13:1-11).

In our Lord's illustration the one who is clean is one who has been
forgiven the eternal penalty of sin. Judas was obviously the disciple
Jesus is referring to who had not received forgiveness from the eternal
penalty of sin and was considered positionally unclean. The rest of the
disciples were clean positionally but had dirtied their feet (to follow
Jesus' metaphor). In this account the one who has dirty feet is a saved
individual who has sinned after salvation. This included all the disciples except Judas. They did not need to be cleansed from the eternal
penalty of sin, as that had already been accomplished. They needed
cleansing from the temporal consequences of sin.

Just as it would be most inappropriate for a person with filth on their
feet to enter a house and fellowship with the host, so also it would
be most inappropriate for a believer, who has picked up the filth of
life (sin) to expect to have fellowship with God. They already have an

appropriate positional relationship. They have not lost their salvation but they have lost something. They have lost their fellowship with God.

If faith alone in Christ alone is the divinely prescribed remedy for salvation from the penalty of sin and condemnation, then what is the divinely prescribed remedy for the sin the Christian commits *after* salvation? One of the most well known verses in the New Testament supplies the answer.

> If we confess our sins, He is faithful and just to forgive us our sins and to cleanse us from all unrighteousness (1 John 1:9).

The first thing we must note is that the Bible does speak of the believer's responsibility to confess sins *after* salvation. The first comprehensive treatment of the subject comes in Leviticus 5-7, and is expanded in numerous Old Testament passages.[28]

The Bible gives the believer both the benefit and the responsibility to confess sins after salvation

---

While there are differing views on the precise nature of this confession, there is no doubt that the Bible speaks of the concept. That must be our first observation. The Roman Catholic sees the need for a believer to make this confession to a priest. Most Protestants hold that every believer is a priest and has the responsibility to make their confession directly to God. But both groups realize that the Bible gives the believer the benefit and the responsibility to confess sins after salvation.

When the believer sins he has not fallen subject to payment for the eternal debt owed all over again. He is not condemned (Romans 8:1). But again, he has lost something. God is holy. And anything of unholiness found in the believer will cause the relationship he has with his Heavenly Father to suffer. You don't bring the stink of sin into the house and expect God not to notice. The believer has suffered a "loss of fellowship" as opposed to condemnation or "loss of salvation."

Some hold that 1 John 1:9 is a salvation verse that presents a separate and necessary condition (in addition to faith) for receiving forgiveness from the eternal penalty of sin. Those that hold this view typically include in their gospel presentation a "precondition" of confessing all known sin prior to exercising faith, with at least an intention of turning away from those sins. But this view is a result of confusing the different purposes of the Gospel of John and John's first epistle.

In his Gospel, John gave but one condition for the receiving of eternal life and the forgiveness from the eternal penalty of sin, faith. On the other hand, the epistle of 1 John was not written to demonstrate to the unbeliever how they might receive eternal life but rather to the believer to demonstrate how one ought to live after salvation given the fact that they already have eternal life.

Decades after Jesus' teaching in the foot washing episode, the Apostle John put the lesson he learned that day in more theological terms. After explaining in 1 John 1:3 that his purpose in writing the epistle was to show believers how to have fellowship with the Father, John continued,

> This is the message we have heard from Him and announce to you, that God is Light, and in Him there is no darkness at all. If we say that we have fellowship with Him and yet walk in the darkness, we lie and do not practice the truth; but if we walk in the Light as He Himself is in the Light, we have fellowship with one another, and the blood of Jesus His Son cleanses us from all sin (1 John 1:5-7).

In this passage John is equating light with holiness and darkness with sin. God cannot fellowship with that which is sinful. His holiness will not allow it.

In his first epistle, John is speaking to people who have already placed their faith in Jesus and have received forgiveness from the eternal penalty of sin. They have eternal life. In 1 John the apostle prescribes continuing confession of sin as necessary, not optional, for continual cleansing and fellowship with God.

This is critical. For if 1 John was written to show the unbeliever how to get to heaven, and if 1 John 1:9 is a salvation verse as some have claimed, then John made a massive mistake in the writing of his gospel. He left out a necessary condition for the receiving of eternal life and the forgiveness of the eternal penalty of sin.

However, 1 John 1:9 is not describing what it takes to receive forgiveness from the eternal penalty of sin. It is a verse, written to Christians, that gives the divinely prescribed remedy for forgiveness from the consequence of post salvation sins. It tells us how we might be restored to fellowship with God after we have done something that offends His holiness.

Preceding 1 John 1:9, in verse 8 and following in verse 10, the apostle makes it clear that believers can, and do, sin after salvation. Anyone who is honest must admit as much. Verse 10 asserts that to deny that reality makes one a liar.

> If we say that we have no sin, we are deceiving ourselves and the truth is not in us .... If we say that we have not sinned, we make Him a liar and His word is not in us (1 John 1:8, 10).

Please notice the phrase in verse 8, "we are deceiving ourselves." Self-deception is an unhealthy practice in all areas of life but is particularly damaging to the spiritual life. As Mike Martin wrote in his fine work on the subject,

> Evading self-acknowledgement of our faults enables us to avoid painful moral emotions: guilt and remorse for harming others; shame for betraying our own ideals; self-contempt for not meeting even our own minimal commitments. We also bypass the sometimes onerous task of abiding by our own values and manage to sin freely and pleasurably. We avoid the need to make amends and restitution for the harm we do. And, above all, we maintain a flattering self image while pursuing immoral ends, often in the name of virtue. [29]

In between 1 John 1:8 and 10 we find not only the remedy for the "filth on our feet" caused by post salvation sinning, but the cure for self-deception.

> If we confess our sins, He is faithful and righteous to forgive us our sins and to cleanse us from all unrighteousness (1 John 1:9).

We can understand this kind of conditional clause this way: If you do "A" then "B" will happen. For example, "If I pay my rent, I will be able to continue to live in my home." (Assuming of course that everyone involved has integrity)

Greek grammarians of a previous generation labeled this type of conditional clause a "third class conditional." Most contemporary Greek scholars, at least in university settings, prefer the term "future more vivid conditional."[30] In this example of a future more vivid conditional clause, I may or may not pay my rent. But if I do, I will get to stay in my home. Obviously, if I don't, I won't.

In the same way, if we confess our sins (we may or may not, but if we do) God will forgive us and cleanse us from all unrighteousness. Again, it should be obvious; if we don't confess then He won't forgive and cleanse us.

May I go back to our Lord's own illustration of the principle? If we confess, Our Lord washes the filth from our feet and we are in a position to fellowship with Him in an appropriate way, in the fullest sense.

Confession is the only condition given by God for the forgiveness of the consequences of post salvation sins and a return to complete fellowship with Him. Please note again, when we sin after salvation, we are not condemned. We will not pay the eternal penalty for those sins. Jesus has already accomplished that.

WHAT IS MEANT BY CONFESSION?

A confession is an honest and open admission to God that what we did was sinful, that what we did was wrong, and that it violated God's holy standard. It is coming face to face with something we have done and acknowledging to God that it was a sin. It is not making excuses before God. It is coming clean with God. When we confess, we are not informing God of anything. We are admitting to Him something that He *already* knows. At its core it is being honest with God.

It is something very personal, never mechanical. And since it is personal and not mechanical, the confessing believer may feel a sense of guilt or remorse when the confession is offered. Let me be perfectly clear: *The feeling of remorse adds nothing to the transaction of forgiveness.* However, in a healthy individual both psychologically and spiritually, if one is guilty then it is not unreasonable to assume that a feeling of remorse will accompany the reality of guilt. Feeling guilty can be healthy if it leads the individual to positive action.

God the Holy Spirit uses feelings of guilt to motivate the believer to examine their actions and acknowledge the sin that caused the guilt feeling in the first place. Perpetual guilt feelings after confession are not healthy. You have been forgiven. God does not want you to constantly be looking in the rear view mirror of your life concentrating on past failures. On the other hand, an occasional glance in the direction of the past can be a motivating factor in not going there again.

Even though God has forgiven us and we have been restored to fellowship with Him, feelings of remorse or regret can, and do linger, often for the rest of our lives. I know a man who caused the death of another person while driving under the influence of alcohol. As a believer, he confessed the sin to God, and he knows God has removed the guilt from him, but he continues to feel great remorse for his actions. The man he killed had a wife, children and grandchildren who miss him dearly. Of course my friend will continue to feel regret. He is human, after all. But at the same time he also feels God's forgiveness and that is what has carried him through this terrible period in his life.

Sometimes it is difficult to acknowledge the reality of our having been forgiven. We admit God has forgiven us but do not forgive ourselves. Knowing we have been forgiven by God and restored to fellowship with Him is an enormous comfort when we have done something we know we cannot undo. And the reality is, we have all done things that cannot be undone or said things that cannot be unsaid. The eternal penalty for those sins has already been paid.

When we (believers) confess those sins to God He forgives us and restores us to fellowship with Him. If God has forgiven us, who are we to deny the reality of forgiveness to ourselves? To my knowledge, the Bible never speaks specifically of self-forgiveness. But the concept of forgiving ourselves is a reasonable deduction from what we know of the principle of God's loving forgiveness.

God's promise to forgive based upon confession in 1 John 1:9 mentions nothing of our feelings. At the same time one would be hard pressed to find a Biblical example of one who confessed a sin in a mechanical, emotion free manner. We do, however, have examples of the opposite. As Ezra confesses the sins of the people he tears his robe, weeps and prostrates himself (Ezra 9, 10). Daniel's prayer for his people in Daniel 9 is hardly emotionless. David said he was "full of anxiety" because of his sin (Psalm 38:18) and his confession psalm (Psalm 51) is full of passion.

Again, our remorse is not a prerequisite for forgiveness. But remorse (or regret) is a perfectly normal response of a psychologically healthy individual to having done something hurtful or offensive to the holiness of God or injuring to another person. It is also a very reasonable reaction, especially when we consider Christ had to suffer because of our actions. Consistent confession that is completely devoid of remorse is not a sign of a maturing Christian, but rather a sign of a spiritual problem. Returning to our Lord's metaphor in John 13, there is a stench to filthy feet. I'm not sure how healthy it is to pretend that is not so.

When we confess, when we admit, when we acknowledge our sin, God forgives, every sin, every time. He is faithful and just. It is not a violation of His infinite perfections for Him to forgive the sinner because Jesus satisfied the righteous requirement of God's holy character with His work on the Cross. As I wrote earlier with respect to eternal salvation, God could not simply "look the other way" at man's rebellion.

If the relationship was to be restored a price would have to be paid. Jesus' death paid the price. Therefore God is justified in forgiving us the eternal penalty of sin when we place our faith in Jesus and He is justified in forgiving us from the temporal consequence of sin and restoring us to fellowship with Him when we confess.

The temporal consequence of sin is a loss of the close, intimate personal relationship with God that we were designed to have. David called it the "joy of Thy salvation" in Psalm 51. All known sin must be confessed for restoration to fellowship. If we know that we have lied to a friend, stolen a bicycle and hate a fellow believer, we must confess all three. If you confess the first two and refuse to confess the hatred because you are not ready to deal with that yet, you have not been restored to fellowship.

At this point one might ask, " What about the sins I have forgotten?" Or, "What if I missed something because I did not know it was a sin?"

The final clause of 1 John 1:9 handles that problem,

"And He cleanses us from all unrighteousness."

When we acknowledge the sins we remember God also forgives the sins we have forgotten or did not know were sins.

Confession restores the believer to fellowship. Repentance keeps the believer there. Repentance is a serious change of attitude about our sin. To remain in a state of fellowship we must turn away from the sin. Confession without subsequent repentance does little effective good. That is why Solomon wrote:

He who conceals his transgressions will not prosper, but he who confesses and forsakes them will find compassion (Proverbs 28:13).

If we truly desire a healthy experience with God we must not only confess our post salvation sins, but we must also turn away from them. If we don't, our restoration to fellowship will be short lived.

All of us have experienced this. We confess a sin, are restored to fellowship only to repeat that same sin a short time later. The answer is not to give up on the process but to ask God in prayer for the Holy Spirit to change us from the inside out. We can ask God to take away the desire we have to commit certain sins and with spiritual growth those sins become less frequent. We never reach a point in life where we do not sin. But we can reach a point in life where we spend the majority of our time in fellowship with God because we confess quickly and repent sincerely.

Confession restores the believer to fellowship, repentence keeps the believer there

---

There is but one condition for receiving forgiveness from the eternal penalty of sin: faith alone in Christ alone. There is but one condition for receiving forgiveness from the consequence of post salvation sins: confession.

We all like to play in the mud puddles of life on occasion. We all come home soiled from time to time. If we know what's good for us we will wash off before entering the house.

Chapter 7 Summary

■ Just as it would be most inappropriate for a person with filth on their feet to enter a house and fellowship with the host, so also it would be most inappropriate for a believer, who has picked up the filth of life (sin), to expect to have fellowship with God.

■ There is but one condition for receiving forgiveness from the eternal penalty of sin: faith alone in Christ alone. There is but one condition for receiving forgiveness from the consequence of post salvation sins: confession.

■ Confession restores the believer to fellowship. Repentance keeps the believer there.

Something to Consider

The spiritual life is one of living in the sphere of God's influence and guidance. When we are living in fellowship with Him that influence is unhindered. But when we sin and walk away from His fellowship our lives will not achieve the potential we were created to achieve. That is why confession of post salvation sins is so critical. Wise living before God includes confession of wrongdoing as soon as we recognize the sin. When we function in this way, we will spend a maximum amount of time living in fellowship with Him and being guided and comforted by the Holy Spirit's empowering presence.

David: A Case Study

❖ ❖ ❖

In the Psalms of David two very different characters come before us again and again. In some of those Psalms there is expressed the sorrows of one who is consistently righteous, suffering the reproaches of the wicked, yet assured of strength in God, and looking forward to that fullness of joy which is at His right hand. In the other Psalms we hear the sobbings of a convicted conscience, a heart deeply exercised over personal transgression, seeking after divine mercy, and granted a blessed sense of the infinite sufficiency of divine grace to meet his deep need.

Arthur W. Pink

❖ ❖ ❖

In the early days of my ministry I was pleased to receive a visit at my office from a very popular Christian psychologist who hosted a national radio program. Frankly, I was impressed and flattered that a person of her stature would take the time to stop by and chat. I enjoyed the visit very much.

When it came time for her to leave and I was walking her to her car, she casually asked me about my children. Like any proud father I was more than happy to tell her a little about Marcia, Bruce and David who were all still very young at the time. When I mentioned David she asked me if anyone else in my family had that name. After I told her no, she pressed me further and asked if David was the name of a particularly close friend. When I again replied that it was not, she came right to her point and inquired why I named my youngest son David. I told her he was named after King David in the Bible. Her response was not at all what I expected. She stopped walking, dramatically turned, and looking me straight in the eye said, "I *despise* David."

"Really?" I responded. "God loved him, why do you despise him?" Over the next few minutes she outlined, in a very animated way, the failures of David's life and her opinion that David did not suffer nearly as severely as he deserved given the magnitude of his sin. In her view, David "got away with it" and she resented the fact that God kept him on the throne after so great a transgression. She surely could not understand why anyone would name his child after such a man.

I found her comments to be personally offensive and I wondered out loud if she had ever read the whole story or if she had ever heard of the concepts of grace and mercy.

David was the greatest king Israel ever had and he is the king against which all other kings were evaluated in the Scriptures. He will remain the greatest until Jesus returns and assumes the throne in the Millennial Kingdom. David was a man of faith, a military hero and the human author of many of the Psalms. And, like Moses, he was one of the most effective leaders in the history of Israel.

As a young man of 16 or 17 he stared down Goliath with the immortal words, "The battle is the Lord's!" With God's help he vanquished that "uncircumcised Philistine who taunted the armies of the living God." David had twice the spiritual courage in his little finger than I do in my whole body. And lest we forget, he was described as "a man after God's own heart" (1 Samuel 13:14; Acts 13:22).

There is nothing you can do to cause God's love for you to diminish

---

Of course, David was not perfect. Several of his sins are recorded in the Word of God along with many of his successes. All those who have even a casual knowledge of the Word know of his adultery with Bathsheba and his murder of her husband Uriah. Most of us are very pleased to have our own failures remain a private matter between ourselves and God. David's failures are out there for everyone to see. However, it is a mistake to conclude that David's life was defined by his failures. It certainly was not. And neither is yours.

David's sin did not cause God to love him any less, nor did his spiritual successes cause God to love him any more. There is nothing you can do to cause God's love for you to change and there is nothing you can do to cause his love for you to increase. He loves His children with a love that will not let us go.[31] This does not mean that God is indifferent toward our sins. He certainly is not. Our sin offends His holiness. But we should always keep in mind that when we fail, God's love for us remains consistent and permanent.

Almost a year after the adultery with Bathsheba and the murder of Uriah, God sent the prophet Nathan to confront David. When challenged by Nathan, David immediately confessed his sin to God. "I have sinned against the Lord" (2 Samuel 12:13). Sometime later David wrote Psalm 51, expressing in retrospection his thoughts at the moment he came face to face with the evil of his actions.

> Be gracious to me, O God, according to Thy loving-kindness; According to the greatness of your compassion blot out my transgressions.
>
> Wash me thoroughly from my iniquity, And cleanse me from my sin (Psalm 51:1-2).

David was a passionate man. He loved his Lord desperately and his confession reflects that passion. He freely admitted that what he had done was evil and he acknowledged that God was perfectly righteous in His discipline.

> For I know my transgressions,
> And my sin is ever before me.
>
> Against Thee, Thee only have I sinned,
> And done what is evil in Thy sight.
>
> So that Thou art justified when Thou dost speak,
> And blameless when Thou dost judge (Psalm 51: 3-4).

He goes on to express the extreme pain of body and soul he experienced as a result of his sins in another of his Psalms.

> O Lord, rebuke me not in Your wrath,
> And chasten me not in Your burning anger.
>
> For Your arrows have sunk deep into me,
> And Your hand has pressed down on me.
>
> There is no soundness in my flesh because of Your indignation;

There is no health in my bones because of my sin.

For my iniquities are gone over my head;
As a heavy burden they weigh too much for me.

My wounds grow foul and fester
Because of my folly.

I am bent over and greatly bowed down;
I go mourning all day long.

For my loins are filled with burning,
And there is no soundness in my flesh.

I am benumbed and badly crushed;
I groan because of the agitation of my heart
(Psalm 38:1-8).

With all due respect to my psychologist friend, those do not sound like the words of a man who "got away with it." On the contrary, they are the honest expression of a man who was in intense pain and knew exactly why: he was being disciplined by the God he loved for violation of His holy standard.

At the moment David confessed his sin he was restored to fellowship with God. He had not lost his salvation, but he lost the joy that should accompany his salvation (Psalm 51:12). For the period of time he had drifted away from God he had lost his temporal fellowship with God. He had "dirty feet" to use Jesus' illustration from John 13.

God's discipline is not primarily punitive but corrective

God knew it was not in David's best interest to travel down that road of rebellion again. So, in order to discourage a repeat of that behavior, He disciplined David over the next decade of his life in a manner designed to get his attention. We should note here that God's discipline is not primarily punitive but corrective. To put it another way God's discipline is not designed simply to punish the believer but to correct behavior. God does not discipline His children in order to hurt them. He disciplines to help them. Yes, it will be painful. But the pain is designed to change behavior, not to injure.

The first episode of David's pain came in the death of the child of the adultery (2 Samuel 12:15-23). David was deeply grieved during the illness of the child but following his death he was comforted in knowing that he would see the child again.

The second episode occurred a short time later when Amnon, David's firstborn son by his wife Ahinoam, raped David's daughter by another of David's wives Maacah (2 Samuel 13:1-19). How painful it must have been for David to hear of the rape of his daughter and the sting must have been almost unbearable knowing that it was his own son that had perpetuated the offense.

Oddly, David does not intervene in the situation and that opens the door for the third episode of discipline. Absalom, Tamar's brother by the same mother, decided to exact justice against Amnon without the blessing of his father. He murdered his half brother and fled to Geshur, the land of his grandfather, where he lived in exile for three years.

After three years Absalom, who David loved dearly, returned to Jerusalem but there was no reconciliation between father and son. Absalom then led a rebellion against his father that ended in his own death.[32]

This series of events occurred over approximately a ten year period and served as a constant reminder to David of just how destructive sin can be. God did not want David to go that way again and as far as we know, he never did. David sinned again, to be sure. But he did not repeat the same sin. The discipline had its intended effect.

David did not "get away" with anything. He suffered greatly. One can feel his pain in the poetry of his psalms. But he did not lose his eternal life. He was not removed from his position as king. And, the promise of the covenant given to him before the sinful incident remained in place (2 Samuel 7).

This truth is troublesome to many people, including the psychologist who visited my office so long ago. It irritates them that David sinned, confessed and was restored to fellowship. They want David to have suffered even more intensely than he did. The reality is that those who feel that way appreciate grace and mercy when it is shown to them but they are offended when God gives grace to someone else. This is sinful in and of itself and is a prescription for an unfulfilled spiritual life. We all need grace. We all need mercy.

God loved David before and after his sin. And God loves you before and after yours. There will be times God disciplines us after we sin. On those occasions, He does it out of love.

Chapter 8 Summary

■ David, the greatest king in the history of Israel and one of the spiritual giants of his day, was far from a perfect man.

■ His sins of adultery and murder are recorded in Scripture and are well known to even the most causal Bible student.

■ David confessed his sin to God and was forgiven. He was immediately restored to fellowship.

■ But this did not mean his sin was without consequences. He suffered the discipline of God for the next ten years of his life.

■ God's discipline is not designed primarily to punish, it is designed to correct behavior.

Something to Consider

When we fail another human being close to us, that person often withdraws some or all of the affection that had previously marked the relationship. This is a common but painful experience and there is a tendency to go through life trying not to fail because we don't want to lose the love of someone we value. We assume that what is true of human relationships is also true of our relationship with God. But God's love is consistent. There is nothing we can do to make Him love us any more than He already does and there is nothing we can do to make Him love us any less. When we accept that truth, we will discover a new level of confidence and comfort in life. We will not take sin lightly. But we will feel secure in our relationship with Him and His love for us.

Forgiving One Another

❖ ❖ ❖

Every one says forgiveness is a lovely idea, until they have something to forgive.

C.S Lewis

❖ ❖ ❖

When we recognize our need for forgiveness from the eternal penalty of sin and we place our faith in Jesus Christ we confidently expect to be forgiven. God has promised forgiveness and He keeps His promises.

When we sin against God after salvation we are quick to confess and we confidently expect God to wash the filth from our feet. This means we are forgiven and there is a return to intimacy with the Almighty without delay and without acts of penance. Yes, there may be divine discipline to discourage us from continuing down a destructive path, but restoration to fellowship is immediate.

But when people sin against us there is often a tendency to withhold forgiveness or to extend partial forgiveness which, it can be argued, is not really forgiveness at all.

Why is it that I am perfectly content to receive God's merciful forgiveness and yet I am so reluctant to extend that forgiveness to others? One could also ask, "Why is it that I so freely accept God's love toward me but refuse to show it to others?"

This flaw in our experience may very well be what is holding us back in our spiritual life. Perhaps you have thought, "I attend church every week. I give, I pray, I serve. But something is missing. I don't feel like I'm growing in my spiritual life." The possibility exists that a lack of interpersonal forgiveness is holding you back. The believer open to receive forgiveness should be open to extend it.

The quote from the British Christian apologist and Oxford professor C.S. Lewis just mentioned deserves to be heard in its fuller context. During the dark days of World War II the government of Winston Churchill asked several prominent Christians to do a series of radio broadcasts to provide encouragement to the people of Great Britain. Lewis agreed and the broadcasts featuring him were later published in book form under the title, *Mere Christianity.* In it he writes,

> I said in a previous chapter that chastity was the most unpopular of the Christian virtues. But I am not sure I was right. I believe there is one even more unpopular. It is laid down in the Christian rule, 'Thou shalt love thy neighbor as thyself.' Because in Christian morals 'thy neighbor' includes 'thy enemy,' and so we come up against this terrible duty of forgiving our enemies. Everyone says forgiveness is a lovely idea, until they have something to forgive, as we have had during the war. And then to mention the subject at all is to be greeted with howls of anger. It is not that people think this is too high and difficult a virtue: it is that they think it hateful and contemptible. 'That sort of talk makes me sick,' they say. And half of you already want to ask me, 'I wonder how you'd feel about forgiving the Gestapo if you were a Pole or a Jew?'
>
> So do I. I wonder very much. Just as when Christianity tells me that I must not deny my religion even to save myself from death by torture, I wonder very much what I should do when it came to the point. I am not trying to tell you in this book what I could do—I can do precious little—I am telling you what Christianity is. I did not invent it. And there, right in the middle of it, I find 'Forgive us our sins as we forgive those that sin against us.' There is no slightest suggestion that we are offered forgiveness on any other terms. It is made perfectly clear that if we do not forgive we shall not be forgiven. There are no two ways about it.[33]

OUR RESPONSIBILITY TO FORGIVE

Several New Testament passages reveal the believer's responsibility to forgive one that has wronged him. The first is the one Lewis just mentioned. It is found in Matthew 6 in connection with what we know as the Lord's Prayer.

> And forgive us our debts, as we also have forgiven our debtors .... For if you forgive men their transgressions, your heavenly Father will also forgive you. But if you do not forgive men, your Father will not forgive your transgressions (Matthew 6:12, 14-15).

Notice the qualifier Jesus mentions, "*as* we also have been forgiven." In the same manner in which we have been forgiven we are to forgive. Certainly this is an intimidating order. So much so that the New Testament scholar Leon Morris wrote, "This must surely be taken as an aspiration rather than a limitation or none of us would be forgiven; our forgivenesses are so imperfect." Perhaps, but we must not take this casually. This is a serious, and too often overlooked, aspect of the Christian's responsibility as a committed disciple of Jesus.

Refusing to forgive others is in itself a sin

These verses appear to give a second and necessary condition for the receiving of God's post salvation forgiveness. In addition to confession we must forgive others. If we refuse to forgive we will live in a state of perpetual carnality. We may confess our sins to God but if we harbor anger, resentment or a vengeful attitude toward another, our confession is functionally worthless. The moment we finish our prayer, if we have not forgiven others, if we retain sinful resentment and anger toward someone else, we immediately lose our own closeness with the Creator. Refusing to forgive others is in itself a sin.

The psalmist said, "If I regard iniquity in my heart the Lord will not hear"(Psalm 66:18). Our Lord picked up this idea as He addressed His disciples shortly before the Crucifixion.

> And whenever you stand praying, forgive, if you have anything against anyone; so that your Father who is in Heaven also may forgive you your transgressions (Mark 11:25).

Our prayers will only be effective when we make them from a heart that is free from antagonism toward others. The one who stubbornly refuses to extend forgiveness, having been a recipient of forgiveness, cannot expect God's intervention as a result of prayer.

Paul teaches interpersonal forgiveness as vital to the spiritual life.

> Let all bitterness and wrath and anger and clamor and slander be put away from you, along with malice. And be kind to one another, tender hearted, forgiving each other, just as God in Christ has forgiven you (Ephesians 4:31-32).

The Apostle strikes to the heart of the issue in verse 32. We have been the recipients of God's merciful forgiveness. It is the height of inconsistency for us, who have been shown mercy, to refuse to extend the same to others.

But that's not all. It is in our own best interest to forgive. Bitterness, wrath, anger, clamor, slander and malice are all symptomatic of a soul that is holding a grudge. Paul says, let it go. For your own good, *let it go*.

Certainly we recognize this as a Biblical principle. But it is also common sense. Psychologists at the Mayo Clinic explain:

> Nearly everyone has been hurt by the actions or words of another. Perhaps your mother criticized your parenting skills, your colleague sabotaged a project or your partner had an affair. These wounds can leave you with lasting feelings of anger, bitterness or even vengeance—but if you don't practice forgiveness, you might be the one who pays most dearly. By embracing forgiveness, you can also embrace peace, hope, gratitude and joy.[34]

Those comments came from secular psychologists at one of the most respected medical facilities in the world. I don't quote them to validate the point but to demonstrate the universal recognition that forgiveness is s good thing and a lack of forgiveness can harm us not only spiritually, but also psychologically.

There are some things that are universally known. You can't not know them. It is apparent that the concept that forgiveness is healthy and necessary is certainly one of them. Jesus explains this subject even further.

> Be on your guard. If your brother sins, rebuke
> him; and if he repents, forgive him. And if he sins
> against you seven times a day, and returns to you
> seven times, saying I repent, forgive him (Luke
> 17:3-4).

Verse three is a conditional sentence much like 1 John 1:9, in that it
is a future more vivid clause. But there is a difference. In 1 John 1:9
the structure was:

- If you do "A" then "B" will happen.
- "If I pay my rent, I will be able to continue to live in my home."

Here it is a bit different,

- If one does "A" the other party *has the responsibility* to do "B".
- "If I pay my rent, my landlord has the responsibility to let me stay
in my home."

Private reproof, repentance with restitution, and forgiveness were
standard doctrines of Jewish piety. The rabbis doubted the genuineness
of repentance if one planned to sin again, but like Jewish legal experts
exploring legal principles, Jesus offers a theoretical case: if a person
genuinely repents repeatedly, you must forgive that person, repeatedly.

The verb *epitimao* means "to rebuke, to reprove, to censure, to speak
seriously, or "to warn in order to prevent an action or bring one to an
end."[35] The last of these options best fits the context here: "to warn in
order to prevent an action or bring one to an end."

The scenario plays out something like this: Someone does something
to you that is a legitimate offense. (Not something that you simply
choose to take as an offense, but a real offense.) You approach that
individual and discuss the situation with the goal of preventing the
action from occurring in the future or with the intention of bringing
the offending action to an end.

The person sees your point and turns from the action. In polite society
an, "I'm sorry about that," would probably accompany the repentance.
It is then your responsibility to forgive the individual. This does not
mean that the action is forgotten in the sense of cognition. It means

the issue is not acted upon further, either in action or thought. You don't dwell on it.

At this point a question may very well have just popped into your head. What if the one who has wronged us does not ask for forgiveness or acknowledge the wrong? After all, if God's mercy toward us is the model, shouldn't our forgiveness of others await the moment they confess their sin or acknowledge the wrong to me? The question is a fair one.

Surely this is the norm. Typically, in normal civil human interaction when one person wrongs another there is some form of apology. It may be formal or informal based upon the level of familiarity between the individuals but typically there is some acknowledgement of wrongdoing and an indication that it is the intention of the offender to refrain from the offending activity in the future. This is the norm.

But there are other occasions when the person who has wronged you does not in any way acknowledge the wrong. There is no explanation, no apology, no repentance. It is entirely possible that the other individual does not agree with you that a wrong has even been perpetrated. What are we to do then?

To maintain an unforgiving spirit is to harm ourselves

If we are wise we will forgive them in spite of their lack of repentance and move on. And by "moving on" I mean to put the situation behind you.

Matthew 6:14-15 mentions nothing about a prerequisite for us forgiving others. It is simply in our best interest to forgive. To maintain an unforgiving spirit is to harm ourselves. It gives the Enemy a constant opening for attack and does nothing positive for our own spiritual life. You will find yourself consistently out of fellowship with God. One day it will hit you like a brick falling on your head that the person actually got to you twice. Once was their fault, once was yours. Their action kept you out of fellowship by *your* choice, it is a self inflicted wound. Life is too short for that.

HARMING YOURSELF

When I was a young teenager I experienced a situation that illustrates the principle quite well. I was 13 years old and had just started going to a new school. On a beautiful autumn day our physical education class was playing basketball on an outdoor court right next to a game being played by some older boys. At one point in the game our ball rolled into the court next door. Since I was the new kid in school I was quickly appointed to go into the older boy's court and retrieve our ball. At first, all went well. The older boys stopped their game as I respectfully (and fearfully) ask them if I could get our ball. But as I bent down to pick it up, things took a turn for the worse.

When I looked up there was one very tall, very mean looking fellow standing over me and who asked, "What do you think you are doing?"

"Just getting our ball," I replied.

"I don't think so," he said, as he punched me in the face, knocking me to the ground.

I was stunned and bloodied by the blow but managed to pick myself up off the ground and again tried to retrieve our ball. But as soon as I reached my feet I received another punch to my face and again, down I went. By now my nose was bleeding profusely and I could barely see as my eyes were nearly swollen shut. But once more I struggled to my feet.

As I rose the guy struck me a third time, almost knocking me unconscious. All throughout this beating no one came to my aid. Not the coaches who were nearby watching, not the other older boys and certainly not the boys who had sent me over there in the first place. When I pulled myself up that final time the very tall, very mean fellow decided that was enough and laughed at me and moved aside to allow me to take the ball back to our court.

In that particular situation there was very little I could do to defend myself. The guy was older and much stronger than I and there was no way I could have stopped the assault without help. But after my nose stopped bleeding and my black eyes returned to normal I swore to myself that one day I would even the score. I took boxing lessons and enrolled in judo classes. I thought about that guy constantly and determined that one day I would pay him back fourfold. I had nothing but hatred in my heart for him.

As it turned out I never saw him again. But I thought about him with anger in my soul for years. Dozens of times I played the scene out in my head: If I ever saw him again I was going to beat him senseless. I wasn't even close to forgiving him.

The truth is, that fellow wronged me once, but every time I allowed hatred to invade my thoughts I hurt myself. He hurt me once. I hurt myself many times. In refusing to move on and forgive him I slowed my own spiritual progress. My life would have been better if I had simply turned it over to God for repayment and moved on. When we refuse to forgive we continually wound ourselves.

PRACTICAL CONCERNS

We must note however, that forgiveness does not mean that you are obligated to continue to put yourself in a position to be hurt, cheated or abused. If your business partner cheats you, you must forgive him but you do not necessarily have to continue to participate in business together. If your boyfriend is abusive, forgive him but don't marry him. If a friend continually takes advantage of the friendship, forgive her and then find someone else to have lunch with.

The more challenging application comes within families. Those relationships are not so easily avoided. But the principle of forgiveness remains. The necessity to refrain from acting against the wrong continues. We must avoid any word, deed, or thought that is hateful or vengeful.

When I am legitimately wronged, whether or not the offending individual ever acknowledges the wrong I can still forgive them. This means that I harbor no ill will toward the individual, that I expel all malice and bitterness from my soul concerning that person and I look at them through a lens of God's love. Not forgiving someone is like drinking poison and expecting the other person to die.

As far as it is within your control, "live in peace with all men."

> Pursue peace with all men, and the sanctification without which no one will see the Lord. See to it that no one comes short of the grace of God, that no root of bitterness springing up causes trouble and by it many be defiled (Hebrews 12:14-15).

The term pursue is the Greek term *dioko* which means just that, "to pursue, to seek, to run after."[36] The image is one of an African lion pursuing his prey full speed across the plain. The animal devotes every ounce of the energy he has to overtake that which will be his next meal. If we are to be committed in our discipleship for Jesus Christ our pursuit of peace with all men should carry the same intensity.

We are to *actively* seek peace with all men. Not passively, but actively. This means we actively forgive and look for every opportunity to restore. We love because He first loved us. We have the responsibility to act graciously toward others because we have been the recipients of overwhelming grace ourselves.

Not forgiving someone is like drinking poison and expecting the other person to die

---

When we forgive, we are not calling something that was wrong, right. We are not saying that it was "no problem." We are not declaring there was no injury. We are not excusing the behavior. But we are following the command and model of the One who paid the price for every sin ever committed, both the wrongs done against us and the wrongs we have committed against God. Let us not forget that last part.

Forgiving each other is not an easy thing.

Forgiveness requires spiritual courage and a Christ like perspective on life. I know people who have been raped and I know parents of murdered children. I have spoken to individuals who were seriously abused in their youth, and to spouses who have been abused as adults. These are not easy things to forgive, but we must if we are to live a life pleasing to God. He forgave, He expects us to do the same. And if you are wondering where you will get the power to forgive, do not fear. He will give the willing soul the power necessary to fulfill this essential command.

Corrie ten Boom was 48 years old when the Germans invaded the Netherlands in May of 1940. It soon became apparent to Corrie and her family that the Jews and others were in great danger from the Nazis and they knew they had to do something about it. For the next four years her family hid the vulnerable Jews and members of the Dutch resistance in their home, which was also a watchmaker's shop. In February of 1944 an informant betrayed the ten Boom family and they were arrested. Her father died ten days later and Corrie and her sister Betsie were sent to the Ravensbruck concentration camp.

There her sister Betsie died on December 16, 1944. It was a devastating blow for Corrie.

By God's grace, Corrie survived the camp and in 1946 began a worldwide ministry that, over the rest of her life, took her to over 60 countries where she proclaimed the message of Christ's love and forgiveness. At a service in Munich that only God could orchestrate an unexpected meeting took place. Corrie described it in her book, *The Hiding Place*,

> It was at a church service in Munich that I saw him, a former S.S. man who had stood guard at the shower room door in the processing center at Ravensbruck. He was the first of our actual jailers that I had seen since that time. And suddenly it was all there—the roomful of mocking men, the heaps of clothing, Betsie's pain-blanched face.
>
> He came up to me as the church was emptying, beaming and bowing. 'How grateful I am for your message, Fraulein.' He said. 'To think that, as you say, He has washed my sins away!' His hand was thrust out to shake mine. And I, who had preached so often to the people in Bloemendaal the need to forgive, kept my hand at my side.
>
> Even as the angry, vengeful thoughts boiled through me, I saw the sin of them. Jesus Christ had died for this man; was I going to ask for more? Lord Jesus, I prayed, forgive me and help me to forgive him. I tried to smile, I struggled to raise my hand. I could not. I felt nothing, not the slightest spark of warmth or charity. And so again I breathed a silent prayer. Jesus, I prayed, I cannot forgive him. Give me Your forgiveness.
>
> As I took his hand the most incredible thing happened. From my shoulder along my arm and through my hand a current seemed to pass from me to him, while into my heart sprang a love for this stranger that almost overwhelmed me. And so I discovered that it is not on our forgiveness any more than on our goodness that the world's healing hinges, but on His. When He tells us to love our enemies, He gives, along with the command, the love itself.[37]

Corrie ten Boom died in California at the age of 91. But her message of love and forgiveness continues to serve as an inspiration to all who have suffered the indignities of man's inhumanity to man.

T.H. Robinson was right when he remarked, "The spirit open to receive love is of necessity open to bestow love." I could add, the spirit open to receive forgiveness is of necessity open to give forgiveness.

Chapter 9 Summary

■ The concept of forgiving one another is not optional in the Christian life. It is a command.

■ If we refuse to forgive, we are sinning and our own spiritual advance will be significantly slowed.

■ When we forgive another person we are not excusing their behavior. We are following Christ's command and example.

Something to Consider

We have all been wronged in this life and we have all wronged other people. It is not easy to forgive others who have hurt us but it is a command from the One who forgave us and it is also in our own best interest. Far too many lives have suffered spiritually because of a lack of forgiveness. Life is too short to waste time, energy and opportunity with an unforgiving spirit. Do not lock yourself in the prison of unforgiveness.

The Unforgiving Servant

❖ ❖ ❖

No one can measure one's indebtedness to God for the forgiveness God has granted. Therefore, there should be no measure to the forgiveness that we grant those who seek forgiveness from us.   *J. Dwight Pentecost*

For judgment will be merciless to one who has shown no mercy.
(James 2:13)

❖ ❖ ❖

Forgiving someone who has wronged you does not come naturally. It is a difficult undertaking and God is well aware of the challenge of forgiving. After all, before He calls us to forgive, He has forgiven. When He commands his children to forgive each other He is doing no more than calling us to follow His example. Our Lord illustrated the principle of forgiving each other with an emphasis on God's view of the process in Matthew 18.

The Gospel of Matthew was written to a primarily Jewish audience to confirm that Jesus of Nazareth was indeed the promised Messiah to Israel. Matthew presents Jesus as the King of the Jews and was very possibly the first of the gospels written.

In Chapter 18 Jesus elaborates upon the concept of life within community. For many the idea of "community" is an uncomfortable concept. But the Body of Christ is a community of believers who are each gifted spiritually for the "common good."

We live, work and worship in and around other people, whether we like it or not. And it is inevitable that when we are around others for an extended period of time the opportunities for offense, even between fellow believers, is a potential that far too often becomes a reality. Being in a family does not exclude misunderstandings, conflicts and occasional hard feelings.

What are we to do when we are wronged by a "brother?" In the context of community, the parable of the Unforgiving Servant gives us the answer. The parable sheds light on God's attitude toward those who are very happy to receive mercy, compassion and forgiveness, but at the same time are quite reluctant to give it.

Jesus addresses the issue of interpersonal conflict

Leading up to the parable, Jesus addresses the issue of interpersonal conflict within community. Jesus lays down a specific course of action for those who desire to heal discord or conflict in a righteous manner.

> "If your brother sins, go and show him his fault in private; if he listens to you, you have won your brother. But if he does not listen to you, take one or two more with you, so that by the mouth of two or three witnesses every fact may be confirmed. If he refuses to listen to them, tell it to the church; and if he refuses to listen even to the church, let him be to you as a Gentile and a tax collector" (Matthew 18:15-17).

As Peter absorbs this teaching he is conflicted. He knows that the Pharisees, as a rule, taught that a righteous person had an obligation to forgive a wrong suffered against them two times. And for good measure the individual stood on even firmer ground if the offense was forgiven three times, provided that the repentance expressed by the offender was sincere. So Peter asks Jesus, "Lord, how often shall my brother sin against me and I forgive him? Up to seven times?" (Matthew 18:21).

Peter, by using the term "brother," recognizes that Jesus has been teaching about life in the community of believers. And he is surely aware of the prevailing view that a willingness to forgive a brother rather than retaliate is a mark of one who is living righteously. Both Jesus and the Pharisees taught this truth. But Peter is confused as to the scale of the forgiveness that God expects of the righteous. Were the Pharisees correct in their assertion that two times was enough but three times would certainly be sufficient to continue to reside in the sphere of righteousness? He must have had his doubts because he doubles the Pharisees' three times and adds one more just to be safe. "Up to seven times?"

Peter, as he often did, serves as the spokesman for the disciples and no doubt wanted to impress Jesus that he had understood Jesus' message in the Sermon on the Mount, "For I say to you, that unless your righteousness surpasses that of the scribes and Pharisees, you shall not enter the kingdom of Heaven." (Matthew 5:20).

Surely exceeding the Pharisaic requirement by 133% would satisfy any possible requirement of righteousness! But Jesus begs to differ, "I do not say to you seven times but up to seventy times seven." (Matthew 18:22).

Once again Jesus is making the point that the righteousness God requires far exceeds that of the Pharisees. In His answer Jesus used Greek term *alla* translated "but." In doing so Jesus is expressing the contrast in the strongest possible way. Not seven times, but seventy times seven. The Pharisaic standard wasn't even close.

God does not put a limit on the forgiveness He offers us

The number 490 is a Hebrew idiom that represents an unlimited number of times. This very likely stunned Peter and the rest of the disciples, but it should not have. God does not put a limit on the forgiveness that He offers us. We, as His children, are expected to follow His example. Jesus then told this powerful parable.

> "For this reason the kingdom of heaven may be compared to a king who wished to settle accounts with his servants.
>
> When he had begun to settle them, one who owed him ten thousand talents was brought to him.
>
> But since he did not have the means to repay, his lord commanded him to be sold, along with his wife and children and all that he had, and repayment to be made.

So the slave fell to the ground and prostrated himself before him, saying, 'Have patience with me and I will repay you everything.'

And the lord of that slave felt compassion and released him and forgave him the debt.

But that slave went out and found one of his fellow slaves who owed him a hundred denarii; and he seized him and began to choke him, saying, 'Pay back what you owe.'

"So his fellow slave fell to the ground and began to plead with him, saying, 'Have patience with me and I will repay you.'

But he was unwilling and went and threw him in prison until he should pay back what was owed.

So when his fellow slaves saw what had happened, they were deeply grieved and came and reported to their lord all that had happened.

Then summoning him, his lord said to him, 'You wicked slave, I forgave you all that debt because you pleaded with me.

'Should you not also have had mercy on your fellow slave, in the same way that I had mercy on you?'

And his lord, moved with anger, handed him over to the torturers until he should repay all that was owed him.

My heavenly Father will also do the same to you, if each of you does not forgive his brother from your heart" (Matthew 18:23-35).

The king in this parable is representative of God and the servants are representative of those who have been saved by grace through faith apart from works. This parable stresses the magnitude of God's forgiveness as the standard for the forgiveness that He expects of those who are His children. Craig Keener writes,

No one can offend our human moral sensibilities as much as everyone offends the moral sensibilities of a perfect God. The parable accordingly underlines the magnitude of God's forgiveness, a point unlikely to be lost on Jesus' hearers...[38]

The king is owed money and desires to settle his accounts. He calls one servant into his presence that owes him "ten thousand talents." This is an enormous sum, one that would be impossible for any one individual to pay back, even if given a lifetime to do so.[39] How this man came to owe this much is an intriguing side issue but the point of the parable lies in the size of the debt, not in how the man came to be in this sad situation.

Ten thousand is the largest single number that the Greek language could express and the talent was the largest unit of measurement available in the culture of the ancient near east. To put this amount in perspective, at the end of the first Punic War (241 B.C.), one of the demands that Rome made on Carthage was that they repay Rome all the costs of the war plus 3200 talents of silver.

The amount was so large and oppressive that Rome offered Carthage a ten-year plan to repay the debt. To further put this in perspective, according to the historian Josephus, the combined annual tribute paid by the Jews of Galilee and Perea to Herod the Great (who had been appointed by Rome to govern the area) came to only 200 talents. Yet the man in this parable owes his king 10,000 talents!

Jesus does not say whether the debt was in gold or silver but either way the amount was overwhelming, and represents a total that the servant could not possibly ever pay back. The representation here is clear. As those who have been born in condemnation (Romans 5:12-21) and committed untold acts of personal sin because of that original condemnation, we owed a debt that could never possibly be repaid.

That is why salvation from the eternal penalty of sin cannot be by means of works but by grace through faith. The magnitude of God's saving grace is portrayed here by this powerful parable.

The king accepts the man at his word that he cannot repay the money and orders that not only he, but also his wife and children, be sold into slavery until the debt could be repaid. As it was impossible for the unfortunate man to pay back the debt when he was free, being sold into slavery only added insult to injury.

The servant then pleads for mercy. This is expressed through his posture (he falls to the ground) as well as his words, "Have patience with me and I will repay you everything." This is, of course, impossible. He owed an amount that could not be repaid no matter how long of an extension the king might grant. But in desperation the man humbles himself and asks that compassion be shown.

The king is merciful and decides to show compassion to the man, not by giving him the requested time to repay the debt, but by forgiving the debt altogether! Given the amount of the debt this was no small act of compassion.

A reasonable person reading this parable would expect the reaction on the part of the forgiven servant to be one of extreme joy and vocal praise of the king. We would think he would spend his time praising the merciful master and tell everyone he knew of this great act of compassion. And, given the enormity of the mercy that has been given him, we would hope that the man would be inclined to show the same mercy and compassion to others he encounters in the future.

Given our expectations, the next scene in Jesus' story is at the same time shocking and convicting. The servant whose 10,000 talent debt had been completely forgiven is owed 100 denarii by one of his fellow servants. This represented an amount equivalent to approximately 3 months wages for a common laborer, perhaps less than one millionth of the amount the first servant owed the king.[39] But in an appalling turn of events, no mercy is shown. There is no empathy, no compassion, no forgiveness.

Instead, the forgiven servant violently assaults the one who owes him the much smaller amount and demands immediate repayment. When faced with the same request he had made of the king, "Have patience with me and I will repay you," the forgiven servant refuses patience, much less mercy, and has the man thrown into prison until the debt could be satisfied. What an unexpected response! Shouldn't the man who had been forgiven an enormous sum show compassion to one who owed him comparatively little?

When the king is told of the utter lack of compassion on the part of the one to whom so much compassion had been shown he is understandably angry and did not simply sell the man into slavery or put him in prison, but had him tortured until he could pay back the 10,000 talents. It goes without saying that it is rather difficult to pay back even a small sum while one is being tortured.

Then Jesus concludes the discourse with a frightening application, "So shall my heavenly Father do to you, if each of you does not forgive his brother from your heart." The forgiveness that the Father demands is genuine, complete and unhypocritical. Failure to forgive others results in discipline from God.

Let us forgive others with the same grace with which we have been blessed

---

Of course, we should remember that God does not have torturers. This is a parable, not a metaphor and the story cannot be taken to teach the precise nature of God's discipline or of His infinite perfections. The language here is designed to shock the hearer into a realization of the evil of receiving God's gracious forgiveness but refusing to give it. [40]

It should not be missed that God considers the wrong we suffer at the hands of a fellow "brother" to be relatively minor in comparison to the way we might see it. If God can forgive us the greater wrong, then He expects us to extend the same courtesy to a brother who seeks forgiveness from us.

The idea that the wrongs other people commit against us are relatively minor in comparison to the sins we commit against God is a very difficult truth for many to accept. But we must understand, Jesus is not minimizing the pain inflicted by others against us. Evil is ever increasing and shocking in this world.

A number of years ago our neighbor's son was brutally murdered in front of their home. The pain his parents suffered was, and continues to be, far greater than anything I have ever experienced. In this parable, Jesus is in no way minimizing their loss. Jesus loved that young man and He loves his grieving parents. He understands their suffering. He has tremendous compassion for them. He gave His own life for them.

As I mentioned in the previous chapter, I have known people who have been raped and horribly abused. I have met people whose whole families were killed by genocidal tyrants. I have spoken to people whose reputations were ruined by purposefully fabricated news stories, which were written simply to achieve news ratings. The evil humans do to each other knows no limits.

No, Jesus is not minimizing our suffering. He would never do that. On the contrary, He is making a very important theological point. If we are ever to fulfill the command to forgive each other we must come to a full understanding of the principle He taught in the Parable of the Unforgiving Servant.

And here it is: When compared with the sins we commit against the holiness of God the evils committed against us are minor, in comparison. Far from minimizing the evil done to us, Jesus is giving us a very practical picture of just how offensive our sins are to God. As bad as the brutal murder of our neighbor's son was, and it was evil and painful beyond description, our sins against God are worse.

It is impossible for a finite being to comprehend the infinite. And it is equally difficult for human beings to completely grasp the absolute moral purity of God. This parable is not minimizing the evil men do to men. It is stressing the fact that no matter how badly we have been wronged, our transgression against God's absolute holiness is worse. And yet, God forgives us. The application: Let us forgive others with the same grace with which we have been blessed.

J. Dwight Pentecost summarized the message of this parable nicely,

> Since mercy has been extended to the servant, that servant was responsible as a creditor to extend mercy to debtors who sought forgiveness. Since we are by nature sinners, we have accumulated a debt that we are incapable of paying. Christ in mercy provided a salvation for sinners. And the one who seeks God's forgiveness through Jesus Christ is mercifully forgiven all debts. No one can measure one's indebtedness to God for the forgiveness God has granted. Therefore, there should be no measure to the forgiveness that we grant those who seek forgiveness from us. [41]

Chapter 10 Summary

■ Before God calls us to forgive others, He has already forgiven us.

■ The Parable of the Unforgiving Servant illustrates God's attitude toward those who have been forgiven much but refuse to forgive *relatively little.*

■ Jesus is not minimizing the wrongs done against us in the parable. He is stressing that our wrongs against God are comparatively so much worse, no matter how bad we have been wronged by others.

■ God is simply commanding us to follow His example.

■ Failure to forgive others results in discipline from God and a stunted spiritual life.

Something to Consider

In my experience, the concept of forgiving each other is one of the most difficult truths for believers to accept and practice. But this is what Jesus demands, and He demands it without apology. He died as a substitute for all of us, paying the penalty for every sin I have ever committed and for all of yours as well. We may think our sins are relatively minor compared to the sins others commit against us, but God disagrees.

We must come face to face with our own need for mercy before we will ever freely give mercy to others. Forgiving others is an outworking of love for God and is a mark of the maturing believer in Jesus Christ. The next time we are wronged and are faced with an opportunity to forgive, let us remember that without God's grace we would still be facing an eternity of condemnation. But because He forgave, we look forward to an eternal future with Him, in a place of no more pain, no more sorrow, no more tears, no more death, where the old things have passed away, where there will be no more need to forgive others because there will be no more wrongs. Thank you, Lord.

Final Thoughts

Forgiveness has, I believe, been the missing link in the spiritual lives of a great number of believers in Jesus Christ. Far too many Christians have failed to forgive past wrongs and have wondered why their own walk with God doesn't seem to be what they believe it should be.

Perhaps the problem is a refusal to engage in interpersonal forgiveness. As those who have been the recipients of overwhelming mercy does it not make sense that we should be merciful in return?

God counts the refusal to forgive others as a sin. It grieves the Holy Spirit. A refusal to engage in interpersonal forgiveness will result in the believer living perpetually out of fellowship with God and with a spiritual life that is less than fulfilling.

God loved each of us before we were ever born. God's love motivated Him to sacrifice that which was dearest to Him, His eternal Son, to pay the eternal penalty of sin so that by grace through faith we might be forgiven.

God loves us with a loyal love, a love that will not let us go. And when we sin after salvation that love remains consistent. He stands ready to forgive us and restore us to His fellowship when we acknowledge the wrong we have done.

Because God loves us He expects us to love one another. In fact, Jesus taught that if we don't love each other we can't honestly say we love God. And He also indicated that the world will know we are His disciples if we love one another. While the concept of loving each other is expressed in many ways, its expression in forgiving each other is certainly among the most important.

An understanding and appreciation of the principles of forgiveness are essential for the believer in Jesus who desires to follow Him in committed discipleship. When we come to this understanding and appreciation we will enjoy a personal contentment in our lives that, for many of us, has been sadly lacking. We will move toward a maturing relationship with our Creator. We will represent Jesus far more accurately. We will be much more likely to glorify God with our lives. ■

Appendix
The Security of the Believer

The Doctrine of Eternal Security is one of the most debated, yet Biblically defensible truths of the Christian faith. This is not to imply that there are not difficult passages for the affirmation of this view. Jacob Arminius, whose name is now synonymous with those who believe that salvation can be lost, actually held to the security of the believer but admitted there were passages that were difficult for him in this regard.[42] Ironically, in this case, Arminius was not fully Arminian. I agree with Arminius recognizing there are some passages of Scripture that seem to imply that once attained, salvation can be lost. But at the same time, the overwhelming evidence of Scripture is that once an individual has placed their faith in Jesus they are eternally secure in their relationship with God.

When we study Scripture and make an effort to consider the truths of the Bible in a systematic way, we must give priority to passages that, when taken in their context, are clear and indisputable, not subject to other interpretations. All competent theologians are in agreement here. It is a basic principle of Biblical interpretation that the less clear passages must be interpreted in the light of the more clear passages. The less obvious passages are not in any way less important or inspired. They are just more difficult.

I am certain that those who teach that salvation once attained can be lost do so from a sincere heart. As I have traveled all over the world teaching literally thousands of pastors and church leaders I have met many fine Christian men who do not hold to eternal security. When we have had the opportunity to sit down and respectfully discuss the issue I have found that the overwhelming majority of them do not reject the security of the believer for strictly Scriptural reasons. Their rejection of this critical doctrine is typically based upon an experiential fear that if they teach people that eternal life, once attained, cannot be lost they would be giving people "a license to sin." They honestly want to hold people accountable for living righteously after salvation and they fear that if a person truly understood that there was nothing they could do to lose their salvation there would be no motivation to live consistently in fellowship with God.

I respect their motivation, however, we must not yield to our fears if there is clear Scriptural evidence for eternal security. It is apparent from the Scripture that God wants us to feel confident in our relationship with Him while at the same time He deeply desires that His children love Him and serve Him. Fear of loss can be a legitimate motivation to righteous behavior but fear of loss of salvation is not a God ordained motivation.

Charles Ryrie once said, "If eternal life could be lost, we are calling it the wrong thing." Ryrie had a good point. That which is eternal cannot cease to exist. Years ago I sat in a seminary class with J. Dwight Pentecost, a man I admire very much. On that particular day he began the class by asking the question,

> "If I were able to give you ten years of additional life, when would that expire?"
>
> We all dutifully answered, "Ten years."
>
> "What if I gave you 20 additional years of life?" Pentecost continued. "When would that end?"
>
> "In 20 years," the class responded.
>
> "How about 100 years of life?" he continued.
>
> "100 Years," we answered, not really knowing where Dr. P (as he was affectionately known) was going with this.
>
> Then he came to his point. 'What if I gave you eternal life, when would that expire?"
>
> "Never," The class acknowledged.

If it is eternal, by definition, it can never end. That's what Ryrie meant when he said if eternal life could be lost we are calling it thee wrong thing.

When a person becomes saved they receive eternal life. Interestingly, the Scriptures teach that all human beings will continue to exist after they pass on from this life on earth. It is just that some will live on forever in a state of incredible blessing in Heaven while others will live forever separated from the blessing of God in Hell. Eternal life is more than just living forever. It is living forever in the presence and blessing of God. Eternal life is God's life.

It should be remembered that salvation is a free gift from God not based upon works or merit on the part of the believer. We do not work to attain salvation, nor do we work to maintain it. The work of salvation in its entirety was accomplished by Jesus on the Cross. To assert that one must exercise faith to attain salvation but work to maintain it makes the individual an indispensable part of the salvation equation and is most unscriptural. God does all the work in the salvation process. We receive the benefits of Christ's work as a gift.

The Woman At The Well

In John 4 Jesus interacted with an unbelieving woman at the well of Jacob. During the conversation Jesus offered her "water" to drink that having done so she would never thirst again. In the flow of the narrative it is clear that Jesus is not speaking about literal water but eternal life.

> There came a woman of Samaria to draw water. Jesus said to her, "Give Me a drink." For His disciples had gone away into the city to buy food. Therefore the Samaritan woman said to Him, "How is it that You, being a Jew, ask me for a drink since I am a Samaritan woman?" (For Jews have no dealings with Samaritans.) Jesus answered and said to her, "If you knew the gift of God, and who it is who says to you, 'Give Me a drink,' you would have asked Him, and He would have given you living water." She said to Him, "Sir, You have nothing to draw with and the well is deep; where then do You get that living water? You are not greater than our father Jacob, are You, who gave us the well, and drank of it himself and his sons and his cattle?" Jesus answered and said to her, "Everyone who drinks of this water will thirst again; but whoever drinks of the water that I will give him shall never thirst; but the water that I will give him will become in him a well of water springing up to eternal life" (John 4:7-14).

When we drink physical water our thirst is quenched, but only temporarily. Depending upon our circumstances we may get thirsty again within minutes. But when we consume the "water" that Jesus offers, the water of eternal life, we will never be thirsty again. This is not something to be passed over lightly. Some believe that we will enjoy eternal life just as long as we are living in constant fellowship with God. If we should stumble in any way we become subject again to the eternal penalty of sin and lose the eternal life that God has given us. But God did not give us a temporary pass into Heaven. He gave us a permanent ticket. Yes, there are consequences to post salvation sinning. David's life was a perfect example of that (see Chapter 8). God disciplines His children. But God does not "send away" His children.

The Power Of All Three Members Of The Trinity

Jesus said,

> "All that the Father gives Me will come to Me, and the one who comes to Me I will certainly not cast out" (John 6:37).

These are words of comfort to us all. Everyone who comes to Jesus will be saved and should have no fear of being driven away by Him. Two verses later Jesus continued,

> "This is the will of Him who sent Me, that of all that He has given Me I lose nothing, but raise it up on the last day. For this is the will of My Father, that everyone who beholds the Son and believes in Him will have eternal life, and I Myself will raise him up on the last day" (John 6:39-40).

The ones who have been given to Jesus are His, and none will be lost. There is confidence and assurance for us in Jesus' statement. It is the Father's will that all who trust Christ will live forever in Heaven.

Jesus' stressed the issue once more in John 10,

> "My sheep hear My voice, and I know them, and they follow Me; and I give eternal life to them, and they will never perish; and no one will snatch them out of My hand. My Father, who has given them to Me, is greater than all; and no one is able to snatch them out of the Father's hand. I and the Father are one" (John 10:27-30).

Again, please note that Jesus gives *eternal* life to His sheep, not life until the sheep disappoint Him. And no one is able to take from Him those that are His. He has us firmly in His omnipotent grip. Jesus is all powerful. He displayed this great power as the agent of the Trinity responsible for creating the universe. (John 1:3) Jesus spoke and the universe came into existence. He can do anything that is intrinsically possible to do. There is no power in existence that is even close to His. It should be evident, therefore, that if we are in the omnipotent grip of God, no one can come close to prying us away from Him. And not only that, Jesus says the Father also has us in His grip. We have two omnipotent beings holding us firmly. God loves us with a love that will never let us go. We were not designed to live a life of fear of failure. Yes, we will sin. In fact, we fail all the time, but our security is not a result of our good character. It is based upon the character and power of God.

The Third Person of the Trinity is also involved in our security. Paul writes in Ephesians 4:30, "Do not grieve the Holy Spirit of God, by whom you were sealed for the day of redemption."

In ancient times a seal was used to ensure security or privacy. In Biblical times seals were typically made of wax and carried the personal imprint of the one whose document or other item was being secured. To break the seal of a document, for example, would be a gross invasion of privacy and if it was a royal document, the offense was punishable by death.

In Ephesians 4:30, Paul borrows this imagery and applies it to the Holy Spirit's ministry in the security of the believer. We are sealed, not with wax, but by the Holy Spirit, until the day of redemption. And please remember, the Holy Spirit is just as omnipotent as the Father and the Son. When He seals you, you will remain sealed forever. Just as nothing can take you from the grip of the Father and Son, nothing can break you out of the Holy Spirit's sealing.

There Is Therefore No Condemnation

In Paul's letter to the Romans he writes of the righteousness of God and our need of it. After his introductory comments he presents three categories of persons that need the righteousness of God: the immoral person, the moral person and the Jew. He concludes that "all are under sin" (Romans 3:9) and "all have sinned and fall short of the glory of God (Romans 3:23). All human beings need the righteousness of God to be rightly related to Him. But how is that righteousness obtained? Not by our own good works, but by grace through faith.

In Romans 3:21-28 Paul asserts that we receive God's righteousness at the moment we place our faith in Jesus. This is what makes us acceptable to God. At that moment of faith He declares us righteous; an event Paul calls justification.

Paul opens Romans 8 with these comforting words, " There is therefore no condemnation for those who are in Christ Jesus." The designation, "in Christ Jesus," "in Christ," or "in Him" is Paul's way of describing one who has been declared righteous and is now in union with Christ. Those who are "in Christ" are no longer condemned. This was a great comfort to Paul and it is a great comfort to me. We are not free from condemnation based upon our own goodness but because we now have the righteousness of God. But the question could be asked, "Can we lose the righteousness of God?"

The answer to that question is a very solid, "no." This is made very clear at the close of Chapter 8 when Paul writes,

> For I am convinced that neither death, nor life, nor angels, nor principalities, nor things present, nor things to come, nor powers, nor height, nor depth, nor any other created thing, will be able to sep-arate us from the love of God, which is in Christ Jesus our Lord (Romans 8:38-39).

Nothing in life, nothing in death, no angelic being, no human being, no present sin nor any future judgment will be able to separate you from God's love which is "in Christ Jesus." It is no accident that Paul concludes the chapter using the same phrase with which he began it. There is no condemnation for those "in Christ Jesus." And there never will be.

But What About…?

As I mentioned in the opening of this appendix there are passages that are difficult for almost every view on every theological subject and the study of the security of the believer is no exception. There are passages that give honest, objective students of the Word some concern when discussing the issue of "once saved, always saved." For Jacob Arminius the most troubling passage was Hebrews 6:4-6,

> For in the case of those who have once been en-
> lightened and have tasted of the heavenly gift and
> have been made partakers of the Holy Spirit, and
> have tasted the good word of God and the powers
> of the age to come, and then have fallen away, it
> is impossible to renew them again to repentance,
> since they again crucify to themselves the Son of
> God and put Him to open shame (Hebrews 6:4-6).

Many attempts have been made historically to explain this difficult passage and it is not my purpose to consider all of them here, but a look at the context of the passage and the purpose of the letter will be helpful in this discussion. The Book of Hebrews is very Jewish in its context. It was originally directed toward first century Jewish Christians to encourage them to follow through on what they knew of the greatness of Christ and to mature in the faith, not falling away when times get tough. As a part of this message, the writer to the Hebrews issues five distinct warnings found in 2:1-4; 3:7-4:13;5:11-6-12; 10:19-39; 12:14-29.

It is generally agreed upon by New Testament scholars that each of these five passages is warning the same group of people about the same issue. So, the two primary questions are: "Who is being warned?" and "What are they being warned about?"

If we consider the language of Hebrews 6:4-5, the person referenced is, one who has been "enlightened," has "tasted the Heavenly gift," has been made a "partaker of the Holy Spirit," and has "tasted the Word of God and the powers of the age to come." It is extremely difficult to see this person as an unbeliever, or as some Calvinists claim, "one who has a professed faith in Christ but in reality is not a believer." No, the individual referenced is a believer. They have been saved. To take this any other way is to leave the boundaries of sound exegesis.

But what is this believer being warned against? There are really only two probabilities: they are being warned that if they fall away they will lose their salvation or if they fall away they will lose something else, but not their salvation.

In keeping with the overall purpose and message of the book the believer is being warned in this passage against falling away from a recognition of the greatness and sufficiency of Christ and, in context, returning to the Old Testament system of sacrifices. Hebrews 6:4-6 stresses that there is a line one can cross from which there is no return. One can, as a believer, so reject the sufficiency of the one who saved them that they can never return. God's discipline will result in what John calls "the sin leading to death" (1 John 5:16). This is not a loss of salvation but a loss of blessing in eternity and a less than favorable evaluation at the Judgment Seat of Christ.

In summary, there are at least ten views on the passage held by conservative expositors. [43] It is not my purpose to explore them all but to give you what I believe to be the most straight forward understanding of the passage. Since the passages that argue for eternal security are clear and the Hebrews passage is subject to a variety of interpretations the best theological method is to understand the difficult passage in light of the clear ones.

Notes

Chapter 1: The Choice
[1]This quote came from a lecture by Walter C. Kaiser Jr. on *The Christian and Old Testament Theology* given at the Grand Rapids Baptist Seminary in August of 1978.

[2] To put it another way, the overall purpose of all of God's self disclosure, whether in nature, in the Scriptures or in Christ is to reveal His glory. His plan to redeem mankind through the death of His Son is a major theme in the overall purpose of the revelation of His glory.

[3] Some have speculated that perhaps a thousand years passed between the creation account of Genesis 1-2 and the account of the Fall in Genesis 3, drawing upon the idea of a parallel with the 1000 year Millennial Kingdom at the end of human history. And while that is possible, it is unlikely. The original couple had been commanded to "be fruitful and multiply" immediately after they came into existence (Gen 1:28). If 1000 years had passed after creation and before the Fall, one would assume that there would be some young ones running around making noise and breaking things in the Garden by the time Genesis 3 begins.

[4] Victor Hamilton, *The Book of Genesis*, The New International Commentary on the Old Testament (Grand Rapids: William B. Eerdmans, 1990) p.190

[5] Allen Ross, *Creation and Blessing, A Guide to the Study and Exposition of Genesis* (Grand Rapids: Baker 1996) p.137

Chapter 2: The Consequences of Rebellion
[6] Norman Geisler, *Systematic Theology*, Vol 3 (Grand Rapids: Bethany House 2004) p.126 Geisler amplifies the principle: "Clearly a sick person is able to receive a cure, just as a dirty person can embrace cleansing and a person in the dark can accept light. In every case, the sinner is incapable of doing these things *by himself* (in his own strength); lacking spiritual life, he needs the aid of the grace of God. *Total depravity*, then, means "total inability to achieve/obtain the solution to our sin by ourselves," *not* "total inability to accept it from God."

Chapter 3: Grace
[7] An example of this is found in the account of the death of the child born as a result of David's sin with Bathsheba in 2 Samuel 12:21-23. "Then the servants said to him, 'What is this thing you have done? While the child was alive, you

fasted and wept; but when the child died, you arose and ate food.' And he said, 'While the child was *still* alive, I fasted and wept, for I said, "Who knows, the Lord may be gracious to me, that the child may live." But now that he has died; why should I fast? Can I bring him back again? I shall go to him but he will not return to me.'" David's first child with Bathsheba died and David is comforted in knowing that while the child cannot return to him, he will go to the child. If this simply meant that David would one day join the child in death, there would be no comfort at all, only despair. But David knows he will see the child again in Heaven. This provides great encouragement and comfort for those who have lost children to death. They are, as Robert Lightner has written, "safe in the arms of Jesus."

[8] Some have (mistakenly) read this text as indicating that the woman will experience great pain in childbirth but nevertheless will have an insatiable desire for intimacy with her husband. A Hebrew professor of mine at Dallas Seminary, Robert Chisholm, who has a great sense of humor, remarked in class one day about the view, "Apart from being totally divorced from reality, it's really bad exegesis." For a full explanation of the exegesis of Genesis 3:16 see Ross, *Creation and Blessing,* 145-147; Kenneth A. Matthews, *Genesis, The New American Commentary Vol 1* (Nashville: Broadman and Holman 1996) p. 248

[9] Expositional, verse by verse Bible teaching/preaching solves this dilemma. When one preaches expositionally and adheres to the message of the text, God's emphasis will be maintained.

Chapter 4 The High Cost of Rebellion: The Death of Jesus

[10] J. Dwight Pentecost, *The Words and Works of Jesus Christ* (Grand Rapids: Zondervan 1981) I am indebted to Dr. Pentecost not only for the information in the above referenced text but also for his class *The Life of Christ* which he taught at Dallas Theological Seminary for over 40 years. The list given is a synopsis from both sources.

[11] While some have argued that Judas was a believer acting out of fellowship with His Master, Jesus declares otherwise in John 17:12, "While I was with them, I was keeping them in Thy name which Thou hast given Me; and I guarded them and not one of them perished but the son of perdition, that the Scripture might be fulfilled." It is highly unlikely that Jesus was referring to Judas' physical death, as Judas was still alive when Jesus prayed this prayer.

[12] Roman legions were rarely at full strength.

[13] The Mishnah was the codification of the oral law which had come into existence by the end of the 2nd century. Even though the Mishnah did not come into being until after the trials of Jesus, scholars agree that the law behind the Mishnah was the standard for the early first century. Under Mishnaic law there were many illegal aspects to the Jewish trials of Jesus. Among them: 1. Mishnah 4.8 states that no one should be judged by one judge alone without other judges present. *Jesus was first taken to Annas, where he interrogates Jesus alone.* 2. Mishnah *Sanhedrin 4.1* stresses that capital cases must be tried by day and a decision reached in the daytime. *Jesus was tried at night and the verdict was rendered at night.* 3. Mishnah *Sanhedrin 4.1* insists that capital cases begin with reasons for acquittal. *Jesus' trial began with reasons for conviction.* 4. Mishnah *Sanhedrin 4.5* requires in capital cases that special care be taken to admonish witness to tell the truth. *The Sanhedrin sought false testimony against Jesus.* 5. Mishnah *Sanhedrin 4.5* also assumes that witnesses will be called for the defense. *Jesus had no witnesses offered on His behalf.* 6. Mishna *Sanhedrin 5.2* stresses that when witnesses contradict each other their evidence is nullified. *This was not the case in the trial of Jesus.* 7. Mishnah *Sanhedrin 11.6* holds that all false witnesses must suffer the penalty that the accused would have had to suffer if he were found guilty. *No action is reported against the false accusers of Jesus* 8. Mishnah *Sanhedrin 4.2* insists that in capital cases, judges with less seniority should vote before judges with more seniority. This is to prevent undo influence on the younger judges by the older judges. *In Jesus' case the high priest speaks first to declare Jesus guilty.* 9. Mishnah *Sanhedrin 4.1* states that a verdict for condemnation in a capital trial cannot be arrived at on the same day as the trial, presumably to allow for a thoughtful decision. *In Jesus' case the verdict was arrived at on the same day (night).*

[14] Deuteronomy 17:6

[15] See, Hebrews 1:8; Titus 2:13; Romans 9:5: 1 John 5:20: John 20:28: Colossians 2:9: John 1:1 cf. John 1:14: John 8:58; John 10:33

[16] Leviticus 24:16, "Whoever blasphemes the name of the Lord shall surely be put to death. All the congregation shall stone him. The sojourner as well as the native, when he blasphemes the Name, shall be put to death."

[17] The Greek text records Jesus using a double negative here. This is a very strong negative in Greek, hence the translation, "You will *never* believe."

[18] C.S. Lewis, *Mere Christianity* (San Francisco: Harper, 1952) p. 52

[19] Pentecost, *The Words and Works of Jesus Christ*, p. 468-469

[20] D.A Carson, *The Gospel According to John* (Grand Rapids: Wm. B Erdmans, 1991) p.588-589

[21] Ibid., p. 597

[22] Presumably, Caiaphas is in view here. While all sin is equally offensive to the holiness of God, certain sins carry with them greater consequences and discipline.

[23] Originally published in *Arizona Medicine* March 1965

[24] Hebrews 13:5, quoting Deuteronomy 31:6, asserts that we need not love money because God will "never leave us or forsake us." If we consider the original context of that promise, Moses is telling the Israelites not to fear going into the Land because God was on their side. Later, in the history of Israel the Jews abandoned Yahweh and were disciplined for it. But even in that discipline, God did not abandon His people. Although Israel is under dispersion at the present time, there is a future for Israel. God may discipline the believer when they sin, but He will never abandon him. (See appendix on eternal security)

[25] https://christcenteredteaching.wordpress.com/category/james-stewart

Chapter 6 The Effect of Sin
[26] Geisler, *Systematic Theology* Vol 3, 250

[27] William F Arndt and F Wilbur Gingrich *A Greek-English Lexicon of the New Testament* (Chicago: The University of Chicago Press 1957) p.438-439

Chapter 7 Confession
[28] Normally when the Israelites committed a sin they would bring a sacrifice to the Tabernacle/Temple, confess their sin and receive forgiveness. Although that was the norm there were exceptions. In Numbers 14, Moses intercedes on behalf of the people had rebelled against God and they were pardoned without a sacrifice. This happened more than once in the Exodus journey. When David confesses his sin to Nathan after the Bathsheba/Uriah incident, he is immediately forgiven and no sacrifice was mentioned. Under the Mosaic Law there were different prescriptions for intentional and unintentional sins and for "high handed sins" (also described as "blaspheming the Lord" in Numbers 15:30-31). The individual was to be driven away from the camp "and his guilt shall be in

him." After the Cross, the sacrificial system of the Mosaic Law became obsolete, as Jesus had provided the final sacrifice. The Old Testament system was a shadow of the reality that was to come in Jesus. The believer in this age is not under the regulatory aspect of the Mosaic Law (Romans 6:14).

[29] Mike Martin, *Self Deception and Morality* (Lawrence: University Press of Kansas, 1986) p. 37-38

[30] Maurice Balme and Gilbert Lawall, *Athenaze, An Introduction to Ancient Greek Book II* (Oxford: Oxford Universtiy Press 1991) p. 193

Chapter 8 David, A Case Study
[31] The Hebrew *hesed* often translated, "loyal love" used a multitude of times in the Old Testament, makes the point.

[32] In 2 Samuel 12:6 David responded to Nathan's parable by saying, "And he must make restitution fourfold because he did this thing and had no compassion." It is ironic that David was disciplined fourfold by God for his sin: First, the death of the child. Second, the rape of Tamar. Third, the murder of Amnon by Absalom. And fourth, the rebellion and death of Absalom.

Chapter 9 Forgiving One Another
[33] C.S. Lewis, *Mere Christianity*, 115

[34] http://www.mayoclinic.org/healthy-lifestyle/adult-health/in-depth/forgiveness/art-20047692

[35] William F Arndt and F Wilbur Gingrich *A Greek-English Lexicon of the New Testament*, p.303

[36] Ibid., p.201

[37] Corrie Ten Boom, *The Hiding Place* (Grand Rapids: Baker 1971) p. 247-248

Chapter 10 The Unforgiving Servant
[38] Craig S. Keener, *The Gospel of Matthew, A Socio-Rhetorical Commentary* (Grand Rapids: Wm. B. Eerdmans 2009) p. 458

[39] It has been estimated that it would take a common laborer 164,000 years to pay back a 10,000 talent debt, assuming all the workmen's wages were applied to the debt.

[40] Klyne R. Snodgrass, *Stories with Intent, A Comprehensive Guide to the Parables of Jesus* (Grand Rapids: Wm. B Eerdmans 2008) p. 73 Snodgrass points out, "Parables must be interpreted as analogies that show pieces of reality but may contain other elements for a variety of purposes. Interpreters want parables to serve up whole theological structures on a platter, but parables are not theologies. They *are* theological , and we are greatly impoverished if their theology is neglected, but they must be allowed to do what they intended and not pushed beyond their purposes."

[41] J Dwight Pentecost, *The Parables of Jesus* (Grand Rapids: Kregel 1982) p. 63

Appendix

[42]Arminius made the following statement about a year before his death in a work called *The Declaration of the Sentiments and the Perseverance of the Saints (October 30, 1608)* "Though I here openly and ingenuously affirm, I never taught that a *true believer can, either totally or finally fall away from the faith, and perish*; yet I will not conceal, that there are passages of scripture which seem to me to wear this aspect; and those answers to them which I have been permitted to see, are not of such a kind as to approve themselves on all points to my understanding."

[43] For a full listing of the ten possible understandings/interpretations of Hebrews 6:4-6 see Arnold Fruchtenbaum, *Hebrews, James, 1 &2 Peter and Jude, Ariel's Bible Commentary* (Tustin: Ariel Ministries 2005) p. 78-87. For an explanation of all the warning passages in Hebrews, see: Herbert W. Bateman IV, General Editor *Four Views on the Warning Passages in Hebrews* (Grand Rapids: Kregel 2007)